Developing Authentic Character

A Biblical Solution to an Optimal YOU!

APRIL SCHELL BLACK

Copyright © 2017 April Schell Black

All rights reserved.

ISBN: 1546860312
ISBN-13: 978-1546860310

DEDICATION

To God Be The Glory!

TABLE OF CONTENTS

Acknowledgments	I
Introduction to CHARACTER	1
CONTENTMENT	4
HEART	38
ATTITUDE	58
REVERENCE	77
ACTIONS	91
COURAGE	109
TRUSTWORTHINESS / INTEGRITY	117
ETIQUETTE / CONVERSATION	125
RESPECT	138

ACKNOWLEDGMENTS

A very, special thanks to my loving husband for your selfless support and encouragement throughout this process. Also, thanks for facilitating the editing and design which helped this book become a reality! Thanks to my beautiful daughter inside and out (Jada) and my handsome and loving son (Joshua). You have brought great joy and fulfillment to my life. In addition, I would like to thank my mother and father who instilled in me to finish what I start among many other jewels of wisdom. Much love to my sister and brother- I know God is well pleased with who you are becoming. Thanks to my entire church family as well as my Pastor and First Lady at Bethel Missionary Baptist Church for the spiritual teachings you have imparted in my life. I love you all dearly! May God continue to bless you!

APRIL SCHELL BLACK

Introduction to CHARACTER

"Being confident of this, that He who began a good work in you will carry it on to completion until the day of Christ Jesus."
(Philippians 1:6)

"Good character is more praised than outstanding talent. Most talents are to some extent a gift. Good character, by contrast, is not given to us. We have to build it piece by piece- by thought, choice, courage and determination." (John Wooden)

Developing Authentic Character is the key to unlocking the door to the mystery of self-sabotage. Commonly, there are certain habits and beliefs that we have that can lead us off course from God's perfect and divine design for our lives. Often times God will not reveal His blessings to us until our character is ready to receive them. The French Critic Alphonse Karr puts it this way, "Every man has three characters- that which he exhibits, that which he has, and that which he thinks he has." I pray that this book will help you examine and develop the type of authentic character that God wants all of us to have.

Luke 6:40 puts it this way: "A disciple is not greater than his teacher, but everyone when fully trained will be like his teacher" (NET). God is not calling us to be greater than the Master Teacher, Jesus Christ, or to be Christ. However, God is calling us to be like Jesus as it relates to us imitating His character.

It is important to note that God is not looking to build up our natural efforts to exhibit good character, for our natural virtues will never come close to what Jesus wants. On the contrary, God is looking to wither up our confidence in the natural man and transform and re-make us on the inside, so that we can seize the divine power and strength imparted in us by God's Spirit.

God is always calling His children to go higher spiritually. Inevitably, there is always a blessing in our obedience. Let us purpose in our hearts and open our minds to allow a fresh revelation of how we can develop true *Authentic Character.*

1

CONTENTMENT

But godliness with contentment is great gain (I Timothy 6:6)

Contentment depends on your perspective.

Some of you may have seen or heard of a phenomenal motivational speaker by the name of Nick Vujicic. Nick is in his early twenties and travels all over the world speaking to millions of people, young and old, about the message of hope. Nick has started schools in third world countries, built hospitals and orphanages and is a successful real-estate investor and stock market investor. You might be thinking to yourself, *wow that's great for Nick; he sounds like he's on the ball.* However, there is one fact that I left out of his biography - Nick was born with no arms and no legs. As a matter of fact, Nick doesn't even have *stubs* on his arms and legs on which to attach a prosthetic limb! At first thought, you might wonder to yourself, *how is he able to live and make it in society?* Or, *how can he possibly be successful?* You are not alone in your thinking.

Nick explained in a recent speech that his mom was a nurse and had delivered countless babies before he was born. After giving birth and learning of Nick's condition she took him to the best doctors she could find. Nick said even though he had great parents he said as a child growing up he wanted someone to sincerely look him in the eye and tell him everything would be alright, and that he could still have a good quality life and truly believe it. Unfortunately, he could find no one that would say that because, after all, at that time his case was so rare no one knew of anyone who had ever been in his predicament before.

When considering Nick's condition, his life may seem dismal and hopeless. On the contrary, Nick's life is anything but dismal and hopeless. Nick learned that with God's help, he had to learn how to encourage *himself*. He also discovered that he had to stop looking at what he does not have and start looking at what he *does* have. Fortunately, Nick has what he affectionately calls "a little chicken foot", which is attached to his torso which he uses to move back and forth on stage, as well as to help him in his day-to-day life. Today, Nick not only is very successful professionally, but he also swims and has a very full and active life. Nick says he now knows that his situation has had a profound impact on countless of lives as he shares the message of hope. He not only has found his purpose in life but he has also learned what it means to have joy and *true contentment*. I believe we can all learn a lesson or two from Nick.

The only way to have true contentment is to allow everything that happens in our lives to be put in the right perspective.

The American Heritage dictionary gives the definition of **content** (or contentment) in the form of an adjective as well as a verb. In the adjective tense the definition of contentment says *"to be satisfied; happy"*. In the verb tense the definition says *"to make satisfied"*.

We all remember from grade school that verbs express a part of speech that means action. I want us to concentrate on the verb tense definition here, "to make satisfied", since this definition means that we have to be deliberate in our efforts and make a conscious decision to be content. I want to surmise to you that contentment in people does not occur just because of any particular set of favorable circumstances, but, in fact, people can learn to be content *in spite of* their circumstances. Apostle Paul said it best when he wrote the following, *"I have learned in whatsoever state I am, therewith to be content"* (Philippians 4:11). We probably have heard before and know by now that there is a difference between the terms "happy" and "joy" (joy and contentment are often used synonymously). Being "happy" is marked by enjoyment of the pleasure of circumstances. In other words, if good things are going on then you are happy and if bad things are going on then you are sad. There is certainly nothing wrong with being happy. However, we want to emulate Apostle Paul and discipline our hearts and minds and make our emotions slaves to us and not the other way around.

The bible also teaches us great truths that we need to learn in order to have authentic joy and true contentment.

Learn to enjoy what God has already given you

To illustrate these thoughts, review the scriptures and quotes below:

- *Rejoice in the Lord always. I will say it again: Rejoice!* (Philippians 4:4).

- *Rejoicing is a matter of obedience to God --- an obedience that will start you on the road to peace and contentment. (Kay Arthur)*

Rejoicing and being content with what God has given us is an act of obedience to God.

Paul's statement in the scripture, *"Godliness with contentment is great gain"* (1 Timothy 6:6) is power-packed with an array of undeniable spiritual truths. *Godliness* concerns itself with our obedience to God's commands and *contentment* concerns itself with our satisfaction and joy in Christ that can only come through obedience to God's word.

The Gospel of John tells us this: *"If you obey my commands, you will remain in my love, just as I have obeyed my Father's commands and remain in His love. I have told you this so that my joy may be in you and that your joy may be complete"* (John 15:10-11). Jesus has given us the antidote for having joy. Just as Jesus maintained that His obedience to the Father was the basis of His joy, likewise, Christians who are obedient to our Father's commandments will experience the same joy.

Jesus says, *"I am coming to you now, but I say these things while I am still in the world, so that they may have the full measure of joy within them"* (John 17:13). As we grow more and more in the likeness of Christ and our character starts to reflect the attributes of God, our level of satisfaction and contentment will no longer be bound by what we have or don't have, but by our level of commitment to God's word.

Some people think that if they can get everything that is on their wish list that then they will be content. Research shows that people who have experienced similar life events whether good or bad can come away with nearly opposite perceptions of life satisfaction, (Chen 1996).

I love funny illustrations to help drive home the point:

There was a family that had twin boys whose only resemblance to each other was their looks. If one felt it was too hot, the other thought it was too cold. If one said the TV was too loud, the other claimed the volume needed to be turned up. Opposite in every way, one was an eternal optimist, the other a doom and gloom pessimist.

Just to see what would happen, at Christmas time their father loaded the pessimist's room with every imaginable toy and game. The optimist's room he loaded with horse manure. That night the father passed by the pessimist's room and found him sitting amid his new gifts crying bitterly.

"Why are you crying?" the father asked.

"Because my friends will be jealous, I'll have to read all these instructions before I can do anything with this stuff, I'll constantly need batteries, and my toys will eventually get broken," answered the pessimist twin.

Passing the optimist twin's room, the father found him dancing for joy in the pile of manure.

"What are you so happy about?" he asked. To which his optimist twin replied, "There's got to be a pony in here somewhere!"

Rejoice in the Lord always. I will say it again: Rejoice!

Learn to use what God has given you and live a purposeful life

His master replied, 'Well done, good and faithful servant! You have been faithful with a few things; I will put you in charge of many things. Come and share your master's happiness!' (Matthew 25:21)

God often reveals His direction for our lives through the way He made us...with a certain personality and unique skills. (Bill Hybels)

One lesson we can take away from the young motivational speaker, Nick Vujicic, is that he decided not to dwell on what he doesn't have or what he can't do and started focusing on what God has given him. At some point Nick found himself at a crossroads in his life where he had to make a decision whether he was going to dwell on the fact that he had no arms and legs, or focus on the great mind, great heart and, as he likes to put it, "great looks" he has. Even though Nick knew having no limbs would be challenging, he also knew that God promised in His word, *"You are my servant; I have chosen you and have not rejected you. So do not fear, for I am with you; do not be dismayed, for I am your God. I will strengthen you and help you*" (Isaiah 41:10 NIV).

God has enabled Nick to be more successful and more contented in life than anyone could have ever imagined. God has the same intentions for us. Jeremiah 29:11 tells us, "*For I know the plans I have for you, declares the Lord, plans to prosper you and not to harm you, plans to give you hope and a future.*" Just like Nick, God has a specific, unique purpose just for us to individually do. Often times God uses our passions, our failures, our disappointments, our talents, our experiences, our personalities and our willingness to be used by God to live out our God-given purpose.

Pastor Rick Warren, author of the book, *The Purpose Driven Life,* notes that a little phrase in Acts 13:36 forever altered the course of his life:

> "It was only seven words but, like a stamp of a searing hot branding iron, my life was permanently marked by these words: "*David served God's purpose*

in his generation." Now I understand why God called David *"a man after my own heart."* David dedicated his life to fulfilling God's purposes on earth. This phrase is the ultimate definition of a life well lived."

So like David in the bible, or Nick Vujicic, we, too, have to make a choice on whether we are going to be a victim or a victor; be bitter or better. Let us choose who the bible says we are, and be victors - living a purposeful life.

Learn not to compare yourself to others and realize that you may already have what you want.

We do not dare to classify or compare ourselves with some who commend themselves. When they measure themselves by themselves and compare themselves with themselves, they are not wise. (II Corinthians 10:12)

"Enjoy the little things, for one day you may look back and realize they were the big things." (Robert Brault)

Comparing yourself to others is futile. It brings about no useful results. According to Li, Young Wei, et.

al., in research conducted with over 8,000 adults, it was discovered that one of the factors that had a major negative effect on people's happiness was the use of comparisons. Constant comparing yourself to other people not only can bring upon such great personal dissatisfaction, but it also can spur on the feelings of jealousy and coveting, which is a sin. We see this played out in many stories in the bible. One story involved Saul and David. Even though Saul was anointed King, Saul became enraged with overwhelming feelings of jealousy and anger when he heard the men singing the song, *"Saul has slain his thousands, and David his tens of thousands"* (I Samuel 18:7).

Another story involved two brothers, Cain and Abel. The bible states that the Lord looked upon Abel's sacrifice and offering with favor and did not look upon Cain's sacrifice with favor. The bible tells us further that, even though Abel was obedient and brought a more excellent sacrifice than Cain, Cain was jealous and became very angry to the point of killing his brother.

In both of these illustrations in the lives of Saul and Cain, we see how dangerous looking at man and making comparisons can be. When we choose to take our eyes off of God and put them on other people, this not only can cause us to enter into sin but it also can diminish our own level of personal gratification for what God has already blessed us with. Typically, being aware of the blessings we already possess and being thankful for them go hand in hand.

Another theme that is commonly expressed in the bible is the consequence of being unthankful. Often times we are unthankful but are unaware of the symptoms that exist. It is important that from time to time we examine the symptoms that manifest in our hearts pertaining to this very consequential subject. Robert L, founder of GreatBibleStudy.com, talks about these various symptoms of being unthankful.

1) *Symptoms of an unthankful heart:*

People who are unthankful will likely have a negative personality and find it easy to complain about little things and/or easily become moody. People with this mindset are not deeply rooted and grounded in a positive or thankful pattern of thinking; therefore, when situations happen that upset them, they quickly forget about the goodness that God has blessed them with and begin to complain and grumble in their hearts. This brings about a negative/pessimistic personality or mood.

A good example of this is when the Israelites would go about complaining even after God had delivered them from the hands of their enemies and provided for them throughout the wilderness journey; however, it was never enough.

2) *Unthankful people are known to be bitter or unforgiving towards themselves, God or other people.*

"In Matthew 18, we see a picture of the unthankful servant who was forgiven of a great debt, but could not forgive his fellow servant of a much smaller debt. If a person is bitter or has an unforgiving heart towards others, then it shows us that they are unthankful for what God has done for them."

Matthew 18:32-35 puts it this way, "*Then his lord, after that he had called him, said unto him, O thou wicked servant, I forgave thee all that debt, because thou desiredst me: Shouldest not thou also have had compassion on thy fellow servant, even as I had pity on thee? And his lord was wroth, and delivered him to the tormentors, till he should pay all that was due unto him. So likewise shall my heavenly Father do also unto you, if ye from your hearts forgive not everyone his brother their trespasses.*"

> 3) *Unthankful people are rarely satisfied with what they have been given and always seem to want more.*

Never being satisfied with what you have is an obvious sign of an unthankful heart. Greed is a sin that causes us to become unthankful for the things that God has blessed us with. When we become greedy, we are thinking about things we don't have, as oppose to the things we do have.

4) Unthankful people don't take care of the things God has given them.

Those who are thankful for the good things that God has given them will take good care of those things - whether it be their mind, car, body, spouse, children, job, etc. Taking good care of the things which God has given us shows Him that those things mean something to us and we are thankful for them. Not that we ever should worship the things God gives us, but we should take good care of them.

Let us not look at other peoples' blessings and try to live someone else's life that is not meant for us to lead. When we compare ourselves to others it means we have placed our focus on ourselves and other people as opposed to keeping our focus on God. It is so important that we keep our minds as well as our eyes looking to Jesus.

In addition, one of the biggest zappers of joy is thinking that you do not have what you think you want. Sometimes we are so preoccupied with trying to get what we don't have and so busy comparing ourselves to other peoples' situations that we miss the blessings we have staring us in the face. The key to continued contentment is not replicating what someone else has or does, but trusting that God knows what is best for us, and that He intricately and divinely designs our blessings perfectly just to fit us. Let us start enjoying what we already have!

Learn to relinquish your will to God's will

Therefore do not be foolish, but understand what the Lord's will is. (Ephesians 5:17)

Do not conform any longer to the pattern of this world, but be transformed by the renewing of your mind. Then you will be able to test and approve what God's will is - His good, pleasing and perfect will. (Romans 12:2)

Getting on board with God's will is the only way to go.

"The Lord has made everything for His own purposes" (Proverbs 16:4). The bible teaches us that as a believer of Jesus Christ our ultimate goal above all else is to glorify God. Everything in the universe is designed to bring glory to God. *"For since the creation of the world God's invisible qualities – his eternal power and divine nature – have been clearly seen, being understood from what has been made, so that men are without excuse"* (Romans 1:20).

Scientists believe that 200 billion stars and many billion solar systems beside our own reside in the Milky Way. Scientists further estimate that the universe—the entire creation—contains hundreds of billions of galaxies – that sums up to hundreds of thousand million galaxies with each galaxy holding hundreds of thousand million stars and solar systems! Now maybe we can comprehend, even if minutely, the level of awe-striking emotional response from King David when he said, *"O LORD, our Lord, how majestic is your name in all the earth! You have set your glory above the heavens"* (Psalm 8:1-2).

One of the ways as children of God we bring glory to God is to live out our life's purpose. The only way we will fulfill our purpose is when we purpose in our hearts to relinquish our will to God's will. Author Priscilla Shirer reminds us in her bible study, *Jonah: Navigating a Life Interrupted*, that our life involves us but is not ultimately about us. She reminds us that giving God significance is the primary role in our daily living and this means more than just receiving Christ as our personal Savior but also giving up control over our lives and yielding to God's perfect divine way.

Some of us live in continual frustration trying endlessly to have things go the way we want them to. Some of us have laid out specific details, roadmaps and timelines for how we want our lives to be. Although there is nothing wrong with plans in and of itself, however, Proverbs 19:21 reminds us, *"Many are the plans in a man's heart, but it is the Lord's purpose that prevails."* Ultimately, we have to wear our goals loosely and always give way to God's perfect will in our lives. We do this by *"trusting in the Lord with all our hearts and leaning not on our own understanding and in all our ways acknowledge Him, and He will make our paths straight"* (Proverbs 3:5-6).

Another concept that Priscilla Shirer addresses is that there is a difference between being an owner and being a manager. God is obviously the owner over our lives and owner over what He has entrusted to us. *"You are not your own; you were bought with a price"* (1 Corinthian 6: 19-20). In other words, we are just the managers over our lives and stewards over what He has given us. As manager or steward, it is our job to take care of what God has entrusted to us, whatever that may be - whether it's our family, careers, money ,time, talent and even our temples (bodies). God has preordained us individually and specifically to care for all the areas in our sphere of influence to bring glory to God. *"Everything comes from God alone. Everything lives by His power, and everything is for His glory"* (Romans 11:36). We do not own a thing. We are simply the branches and God is the vine and we depend on Him for our very life source for living.

Learn to meditate on positive things

*Finally, brothers, whatever is true, whatever is noble, whatever is right, whatever is pure, whatever is lovely, whatever is admirable – if anything is excellent or praiseworthy – think about such things. (*Philippians 4:8*)*

*The things we think are the things that feed our souls. If we think on pure and lovely things, we shall grow pure and lovely like them; and the converse is equally true. (*Hannah Whitall Smith*)*

The bible clearly states that *"God's ways are higher than our ways and God's thoughts are higher than our thoughts"* (Isaiah 55:9). That is why, in order to meditate on what the Word says (which is anything that is *"true, noble, right, pure, lovely, admirable, excellent and praiseworthy"* (Philippians 4:8), we must adopt the mind of Christ. However, we cannot adopt the mind of Christ in our own strength. As believers our minds more than ever before are under constant attack and are inundated and exposed to the worlds ideals. Most television shows and even commercials now are filled with the recurring themes of sexual immorality, rage, drunkenness, greed, pride, lust, envy, laziness, harshness, strife, and the most common but not always the most recognizable to ourselves, selfishness. All of these fleshly desires that the world encourages, the bible discourages. The bible calls it *"earthly, sensual and devilish behavior"* (James 3:15). As Christians, we have to be mindful that conforming to the world's systems of beliefs and values means that we are complying to a world that is dominated by Satan. John 14:18-19 says, *"If the world hates you, keep in mind that it hated me first. If you belong to the world, it would love you as its own. As it is, you do not belong to the world, but I have chosen you out of the world. That is why the world hates you"*. In order not to fall prey of the demonic schemes we have to renew our minds daily and walk in the Spirit. Galatians 5:16-18 says, *"So I say live by the Spirit, and you will not gratify the desires of the sinful nature. For the sinful nature desires what is contrary to the Spirit, and the Spirit what is contrary to the sinful nature. They are in conflict with each other, so that you do not do what you want. But if you are led by the spirit, you are not under law"*. Moreover, we have to remember to, *"Be not conformed to this world: but be ye transformed by the renewing of your mind, that ye may prove what is that good, and acceptable, and perfect will of God"* (Romans 12:2). Just to recapitulate God's truths, in order to meditate on positive things and adopt the mind of Christ, we must renew our minds with the word of God daily, walk in the Spirit and refuse to conform to this present age (the world).

Learn not to dwell on past failures/regrets

"Not that I have already obtained all this, or have already been made perfect, but I press on to take hold of that for which Christ Jesus took hold of me. Brothers, I do not consider myself yet

to have taken hold of it. But one thing I do: Forgetting what is behind and straining toward what is ahead, I press on toward the goal to win the prize for which God has called me heavenward in Christ Jesus. (Philippians 3:12-14)

"Never yield to gloomy anticipation. Place your hope and confidence in God. He has no record of failure." (author unknown)

"If you can forgive the person you were, accept the person you are, and believe in the person you will become, you are headed for joy. So celebrate your life." (Barbara Johnson)

The Serenity Prayer says it best: *God grant me the serenity to accept the things I cannot change; courage to change the things I can; and wisdom to know the difference.* Apostle Paul encourages us not to dwell on past faults and failures for we cannot change the past, but he tells us to press toward the prize in which God has called us heavenward. According to MacArthur Bible Commentary, in this illustration that Paul gives in Philippians 3, he uses the analogy of a runner to describe the process of Christian maturity. The believer has not reached his goal of Christlikeness, but like a runner in a race, he must continue to pursue it. God knows we were made from dust and spiritual perfection will only come when we get our new bodies in heaven. In addition, when we experience seasons of failure and learn from it, we become better for it. God is just as concerned about our going through the process as He is about our getting to our promise lands. God knows that it is a process to shape and mold us into who He wants us to be. Often times it is through our failures that we learn how to be more loving, more kind, more generous, more forgiving and yes, even more joyful and content. It is not until we have learned to completely humble ourselves and surrender our lives to the Lord that He can fully use us.

When we come to an end of ourselves, the beginning of a beautiful transformation takes place. Moreover, when we strive to exhibit the character and attributes of Christlikeness through the power and help of the Holy Spirit, not only will our lives be divinely affected for the better but the lives around us as well.

Let us remember whether it is our past failures or sin, or future transgressions, *"if we confess our sins He is faithful and just and will forgive us our sins and purify us from all unrighteousness"* (1 John 1:9). Also, let us remember if Jesus came to convict us of sin and not to condemn us, then we should not condemn ourselves. This only robs us from our contentment.

Learn to take your mind off of yourself

"Since, then, you have been raised with Christ, set your hearts on things above, where Christ is seated at the right hand of God. Set your minds on things above, not on earthly things." (Colossians 2:15)

I've given up reading books. I find it takes my mind off myself."
(Oscar Levant)

There is nothing that robs a person's joy more than a person who is self-centered rather than God-centered. Oftentimes we are self-centered because we cannot take our minds off of ourselves. It has been estimated that human beings average about 50,000 thoughts per day. Interestingly, many of these thoughts are said to be focused on self. Unfortunately, many of these thoughts are habitual negative thoughts that are played out over and over again in our minds. You can just imagine that, even if subconsciously, we repeat negative thought content on a repetitive basis in our minds about ourselves or about our circumstances, that this would have a serious effect on our level of joy and contentment.

We have to learn to take on the mind of Christ. As soon as negative thoughts enter into our minds, we need to cast them out quickly, before it has time to marinate and formulate into a lengthy meditation. The sooner we catch and cast these negative thoughts out of our minds, the less effect it has on the way that we feel.

II Corinthians 10:5 tells us, *"We demolish arguments*

and every pretension that sets itself up against the knowledge of God, and we take captive every thought to make it obedient to Christ." The only way to true contentment regarding this matter is that we guard our minds, regulate our thoughts and keep our minds stayed on Christ. Staying in God's word is key!

Setting our minds on things above and not on earthly things helps us keep our Christian lives in perspective. We might feel that we are protecting ourselves or protecting "what's rightly ours" by concentrating so heavily on self, but, in fact, the opposite result occurs. The effects are that we push people away and we oftentimes forfeit our own blessings when we are self-centered. The bible tells us, *But seek ye first the kingdom of God and His righteousness and all these things shall be added unto you*, (Matthew 6:33). Oftentimes, we have the cart before the horse; we want to do things our way or the world's way and expect divine blessings. God's economy operates differently from man's economy. Tim Gilligan and Ethan Pope says it best:

- In man's economy…in order to receive…you take -
- In God's economy…in order to receive…you give!
- Man's economy depends on manipulation -
- God's economy counts on favor!
- Man's economy is natural -
- God's economy is super-natural!
- In Man's economy…little runs out -
- In God's economy…little becomes much (multitudes are fed and there are leftovers)!
- In Man's economy…the goal is to get ahead -
- In God's economy…the goal is to be a blessing!
- In man's economy…you try to make a living -
- In God's economy…you try to make a difference!
- In man's economy… we want to be served -
- In God's economy…we want to serve others!
- In man's economy… we spend our life acquiring things -

- In God's economy…we spend our life serving God!
- *In man's economy…we keep our minds on self -*
- *In God's economy…we keep our minds on God!"*

Learn to be thankful

"Be joyful always; pray continually; give thanks in all circumstances, for this is God's will for you in Christ Jesus." (I Thessalonians 5:16-18)

"Let the peace of Christ rule in your hearts, since as members of one body you were called to peace. And be thankful." (Colossians 3:15)

In the book *Conversational Peace: The Power of Transformed Speech*, the author Mary A Kassian informs us that *Charis* is a Greek word for *thanks*. It has the same root that is translated *grace*. Charis means a disposition of kindness, favor and grace on the part of the giver; and Thanks refers to respect and homage on the part of the receiver. Conceptually, the two go hand in hand.

God's *Charis* flowing into us causes us to overflow with *Charis*. As a result, we become characterized by a disposition that is kind and gracious. That is why we are able to "*give thanks for everything* (Ephesians 5:20); *everyone* (I Timothy 2:1) and "*in all circumstances*" (I Thessalonians 5:18).

Therefore, our level of gratitude shows up in our everyday actions. Our conversations with people, our attitudes toward others as well as our attitudes toward our circumstances illuminate greatly the level of thankfulness, or Charis, we have in our hearts. The bible speaks of countless examples of people not having a thankful heart. The bible also shows us how God responds to those who do not have a Charis disposition. For example, because of the Israelites' constant murmuring and complaining, their consequence was prolonged hardship in the wilderness. Many biblical scholars agree that the Israelites journey to the promise land could have taken only 40 days; however, because of their murmuring and complaining attitudes, their blessings were prolonged, and the journey took them *40 years* to reach the promised blessing of the Lord! We have to ask ourselves how many of our blessings have been cut off or prolonged because of an attitude of murmuring, complaining and ungratefulness? Numbers 11:1 tells us this, *"And when the people complained, it displeased the LORD; and the LORD heard it, and His anger was kindled…"*

As Christians we often like to put sin in certain categories of weight much like we categorize items we purchase from the store and determine whether it is a big ticket item or a small ticket item. The bible teaches that there are no big or little sins. *"For whoever keeps the whole law and yet stumbles at just one point is guilty of breaking all of it"* (James 2:10). Sin is sin and murmuring is a sin. *"Do all things without complaining and disputing, that you may become blameless and harmless, children of God without fault in the midst of a crooked and perverse generation, among whom you shine as lights in the world"* (Philippians 2:14-15).

The opposite of complaining is to applause - to be content, be happy, praise and approve. Although God calls us as Christians to have joy, contentment and thankfulness in our hearts, it is certainly not always easy, especially when we are going through various trials. However, nothing more destroys our witness as Christians than when we grumble and complain. We have to rest assure that God has a perfect divine reason for everything.

We may not ever fully understand all of God's decisions nevertheless the bible teaches us that God's ways are higher than our ways and God's thoughts are higher than our thoughts. One thing is for sure "that in all things God works for the good of those who love Him, who have been called according to His purpose" (Romans 8:28). So as we continue on this Christian journey let us not murmur rather let us be content in life. Let us be thankful for everything and let us be characterized as Christians by a spirit of thankfulness

(Charis).

2

HEART

"As water reflects a face, so a man's heart reflects the man."
(Proverbs 27:19)

"Above all else, guard your heart, for it is the wellspring of life."
(Proverbs 4:23)

For many of us when we look at a mirror we notice every minute detail of what is going on with our faces as well as our bodies. Often times, we pay close attention to whether our hair is just the way we want it and if our eyebrows are becoming too bushy. We also notice if new hairs are growing in places we do not want them to, if new bumps or moles are popping up and, God forbid, if new wrinkles appear. Nonetheless, are we examining just as closely to what is on the inside of us as we do to what is on the outside? It is imperative that we are attentive to the changes we see appearing in our thoughts, our words, our actions and even our reactions. We know that people judge us by our outwardly behavior, but the bible tells us that God judges the thoughts and attitudes of our *hearts* (Hebrews 4:12).

Since we know that God places great value on what is in our hearts, we have to keep close watch and guard our hearts with purposeful intention and adhere to every instruction God gives us. Moreover, what is in our hearts has a direct impact on our blessings. Jeremiah 17:10 tells us that, *"I the Lord search the heart and examine the mind, to reward a man according to his conduct, according to what his deeds deserve."*

Let us examine what the Lord has to say about our hearts.

It is important to God that we have a pure *heart*

"Blessed are the pure in heart, for they will see God." (Matthew

5:8)

Purity does not mean perfection. However, as Christians, we should grow in purity. There are three spiritual stages of development in God's plan for His children. The three stages include:

a) <u>Justification</u> which only Christ can justify us through His death, burial and resurrection for the atoning of our sins;

b) <u>Sanctification</u> is the second stage. As Christians we go through the sanctification process with the help of the Holy Spirit. Sanctification means to be set apart or to be made holy. The Holy Spirit helps us with the progression of becoming pure and more like Christ. Philippians 2:12-13 tells us to *"continue to work out your salvation with fear and trembling, for it is God who works in you to will and to act according to His good purpose."* As long as we are in our mortal bodies and as long as we live on this earth we will be working out our soul salvation through the sanctification process;

c) <u>Glorification</u> is the third stage. We will not be glorified until after Jesus returns. John states that, *"when He shall appear we shall be like Him* (I John 3:2). Also, Paul tells us, *"For this corruptible must put on incorruption and this mortal must put on immortality* (I Corinthians 15:53).

When we draw close to God by studying God's Word more, as well as praying and serving God, this signifies our yearning and desire to pursue God's holiness. This pursuit of God's holiness shows our genuine acceptance of Christ as our Lord and Savior and our genuine willingness to let God shape and mold us into the likeness of Christ. No man can make himself pure by obeying laws but through Jesus Christ and the power of the Holy Spirit that works within us as Christians we can live as overcomers and have a heart that is pleasing to God.

It is important to God that we know that our *hearts* can deceive us

"The heart is deceitful above all things and beyond cure. Who can understand it? (Jeremiah 17:9)

Our physical heart is located and protected underneath the rib cage, left of the breastbone and in between the lungs. Additionally, many of us further protect our physical hearts by eating properly, exercising and getting enough rest. As we strive to protect our physical hearts to ensure that it functions properly, we must also be alert and guard our hearts with all diligence to make certain that our spiritual and emotional hearts work and function properly as well. We place ourselves in a vulnerable state and we are susceptible to being deceived by our own hearts when we do not guard our hearts vigilantly.

In the book, *My Utmost for His Highest*, author Oswald Chambers says, *"Much of our distress as Christians comes not because of sin but because we are ignorant of the laws of our own nature."* In other words, as Christians, we have three enemies to contend with - the world, the devil and the flesh. Interestingly, the flesh (which is our carnal nature) and the spirit are in constant war with each other. Consequently, we have to be careful about adopting the popular adage that tells us to "follow your heart" as part of our philosophy. The bible says, *"He who trusts in his own heart is a fool, but he who walks wisely will be delivered"* (Proverbs 28:26). If we are not careful, we can allow our unreliable hearts to lead us in getting involved in selfish and sinful situations and making decisions based off of our fickle feelings rather than sound Godly truths. Instead of following our hearts, we must direct our hearts in the way of the Lord, which is through God's Word.

In addition, Oswald Chambers also suggest that before we should allow an emotion to have its way, we should first test to see if the outcome glorifies God. Even though we may strongly feel in our hearts a certain way we have to examine to see if we are operating in the flesh or in the Spirit. If we are not ruled by the Holy Spirit, our hearts and minds will desire to please the flesh. Consequently, the outcome to feeding the flesh leads to destruction.

Fortunately, God gives us scripture to keep us from being entangled by a deceiving heart. Read the following scriptures below as if you have never read them before.

1. <u>Ephesians 6:11-18:</u> *"Put on the full armor of God so that you can take your stand against the devil's schemes. For our struggle is not against flesh and blood, but against the rulers, against the authorities, against the powers of this dark world and against the spiritual forces of evil in the heavenly realms. Therefore put on the full armor of God, so that when the day of evil comes, you may be able to stand your ground, and after you have done everything, to stand. Stand firm then, with the belt of truth buckled around your*

waist, with the breastplate of righteousness in place, and with your feet fitted with the readiness that comes from the gospel of peace. In addition to all this, take up the shield of faith, with which you can extinguish all the flaming arrows of the evil one. Take the helmet of salvation and the sword of the Spirit, which is the word of God. And pray in the spirit on all occasions with all kinds of prayers and request. With this in mind, be alert and always keep on praying for all the saints."

2. <u>2 Corinthians 10:5</u>: *"We demolish arguments and every pretension that sets itself up against the knowledge of God, and we take captive every thought to make it obedient to Christ."*

3. <u>James 1:26</u>: *"If anyone thinks he is religious and does not bridle his tongue but deceives his heart, this person's religion is worthless."*

4. <u>James 1:22</u>: *"Do not merely listen to the word, and so deceive yourselves. Do what it says.*

5. <u>Proverbs 23:17</u>: *"Do not let your heart envy sinners, but always be zealous for the fear of the Lord."*

6. Proverbs 23:19: *"Listen, my son, and be wise, and keep your heart on the right path."*
7. Proverbs 23:26: *"My son, give me your heart and let your eyes keep to my ways."*
8. 1 Kings 8:61: *"But your hearts must be fully committed to the Lord our God, to live by his decrees and obey his commands, as at this time."*
9. James 4:8: *"Come near to God and He will come near to you. Wash your hands, you sinners, and purify your hearts, you double minded."*
10. James 5:8: *"You also, be patient. Establish your hearts, for the coming of the Lord is at hand."*

It is important to God that we know that a gentle and humble *heart* will have a restful soul

---

"Come to me, all you who are weary and burdened, and I will give you rest. Take my yoke upon you and learn from me, for I am gentle and humble in heart, and you will find rest for your soul"
(Matthew 11:28)

How can we find rest for our souls in a world that

has so much unrest? There are continuous wars; countless, senseless killings; people who thrive on taking advantage of the weak; economic uncertainty; indefinite number of diseases; national and international disunity as well as family divisions. However, in Matthew 11:28 Jesus acknowledges that He exhibits the characteristics of being gentle and humble in heart, and if we exercise those same qualities and learn from Him, Jesus promises that we will find rest. Jesus urges us to take His yoke upon us. Roget's II Dictionary and Thesaurus tells us that yoke means *"to bring or come together into a united whole; to conjoin, connect or unite"*. There are some yokes we put on ourselves that causes physical agony and mental anguish. However, when we become connected with Christ, we learn that Jesus's yoke is easy and light. It is when we start to exhibit Jesus's characteristics of being gentle and humble that we will find rest for our souls. Mother Teresa wrote, *"The only thing Jesus has asked us to be is meek and humble of heart, and to do this, he has taught us to pray. He has put 'meek' first. From that one word comes gentleness, thoughtfulness, simplicity, generosity, truthfulness. For whom? For one another. Jesus put 'humility' after meekness. We cannot love one another unless we hear the voice of God in our hearts."*

According to Mother Teresa these are the few ways we can practice humility:

- To speak as little as possible of oneself
- To mind one's own business.
- Not to want to manage other people's affairs.
- To accept contradiction and correction cheerfully.
- To pass over the mistakes of others.
- To accept insults and injuries.
- To accept being slighted, forgotten, and disliked.
- Not to seek to be specially loved and admired.
- To be kind and gentle even under provocation.
- Never to stand on one's dignity.
- To yield in discussion even though one is right.
- To choose always the hardest." (*A Life for God*, 65)

It is important to God that we understand that our hearts are where our treasure is

"For where your treasure is, there your heart will be also" (Matthew 6:21).

A man's heart will be on what he treasures most. It will either be on the things of this world or on heavenly things. Often times the things of this world include material possessions. The bible makes it clear that we cannot serve two masters. *"No one can serve two masters, for either he will hate the one and love the other, or he will be devoted to the one and despise the other. You cannot serve God and money"* (Matthew 6:24). We have to choose who and what we are willing to serve. Understandably, we need certain earthly possessions to survive, and enjoying the blessings God has given us even if it is in abundance is not a sin. The problem comes in when we have placed higher importance on the earthly treasures than we do the heavenly treasures. When our hearts are supremely engaged in obtaining riches of this world, God recognizes that we are in danger of making these earthly possessions our God. God says in His word, *"Love the Lord your God with all your heart and with all your soul and with all your mind and with all your strength"* (Mark 12:30), and He is not willing to share us with the world.

It is important to God that we understand that sin originates from the *heart*

"For out of the heart come evil thoughts, murder, adultery, sexual immorality, theft, false testimony, slander" (Matthew 15:19)

Jesus continues to teach the disciples the simple but poignant truths about how it is not what is on the outside that makes us unclean, *"but the evil that is in a man's heart is what makes us unclean"* (Matthew 15:16-18). The seed of sin starts in the heart before evil manifests itself through words or actions. That is why we must pray the prayer King David prayed, *"Create in me a pure heart, O God, and renew a steadfast (right) spirit within me"* (Psalm 51:10). When David used the word *"create"*, he gave recognition that the only way he was to have a pure heart was that God, the Creator of all things, would have to create the pure heart in him. The word *renew* indicates that David was at one time in the right spirit, but slid back into a place of sin and now wants to be restored. Just like David, we also can pray the prayer given in Psalm 51:10, and God, our Creator, can create in us pure hearts and renew in us a right spirit within us and He is willing to grant us a willing spirit to sustain us.

It is important to God that we understand that forgiveness comes from the heart

"Let all bitterness and wrath and anger and clamor and slander be put away from you, along with all malice. Be kind to one another, tenderhearted, forgiving one another, as God in Christ forgave you." (Ephesians 4:31-32)

"For if you forgive others their trespasses, your heavenly Father will also forgive you." (Matthew 6:14).

As long as we live on this earth, we will be faced with what we may consider unwarranted, sometimes hurtful, behavior or mistreatment from others toward us. It is not always easy to ignore a wrong that has been done to us, but when we see a situation from God's perspective, this helps us forgive more easily. It is because of the divine miracle of grace, the sacrificial agony of the cross that as Christians our sins are forgiven. Let us offer that same grace to someone else. We cannot forgive in the flesh, but through the help of the Holy Spirit, and love and appreciation to Jesus Christ, our Lord, lets us learn to forgive one another. Below are some poignant quotes about forgiveness:

> *Forgiveness is unlocking the door to set someone free and realizing you were the prisoner.* -Max Lucado

> *It really doesn't matter if the person who hurt you deserves to be forgiven. Forgiveness is a gift you give yourself. You have things to do and you want to move on.* -Author Unknown

> *Forgiveness is not an emotion. Forgiveness is an act of the will, and the will can function regardless of the temperature of the heat.* -Corrie ten Boom

> *We cannot out-sin God's ability to forgive us.* -Beth Moore

It is important to God that we understand that what's stored in our *hearts* will come out in our deeds and words

---

"The good man brings good things out of the good stored up in his heart, and the evil man brings evil things out of the evil stored up in his heart. For out of the overflow of his heart his mouth speaks."
(Luke 6:45)

Most often, when we serve God and exercise good deeds, it is out of the overflow of a superabundant devotional life. When we become Christians, our old nature becomes new. Our new nature, or God's spirit within us, understands our call as Christians, and wants to serve and do good deeds out of sheer love for the Lord and thankfulness for all He has done in our lives. If we do not have a quality devotional life, we can either lack the urge to serve God or our service can become self-serving. Jeremiah 17:10 tells us that when God gets ready to reward us for our conduct and deeds, He first examines our hearts and minds and then rewards us based on our motives. Our motives and our hearts are intimately connected, and our motives are where our treasures lie. Much like a treasure chest is used to store valuable treasures, our hearts are used to store the truthfulness of how we really feel.

Jesus also warns us that whatever is stored in our hearts will eventually come out in our words. *"A good person produces good things from the treasury of a good heart, and an evil person produces evil things from the treasury of an evil heart. What you say flows from what is in your heart"* (Luke 6:45).

Spending time with God is key to having pure motives as well as having a pure heart, so that not only will our actions be pleasing to God but our words as well.

It is important to God that we understand that a person that bears good seed is a person with a noble and good *heart*

"But the seed on good soil stands for those with a noble and good heart, who hear the word, retain it, and by persevering produce a crop." (Luke 8:15)

God often uses the example of seeds in the bible to illustrate many lessons He wants us to understand. Interestingly, seeds often represent potential for great development and growth. If we look at seeds in the natural, acorn seeds grow into very large oak trees, and the seeds of redwood trees, which are very small seeds, grow to extraordinary height and live for centuries. As Christians we are the Spiritual seed of Abraham which makes us heirs of the promises of God. *"If you belong to Christ, then you are Abraham's seed, and heirs according to the promise"* (Galatians 3:29). In the eyes of God Abraham was considered a pillar of faith because of Abraham's belief in God and obedience to God.

Just like Abraham produced good seed, we can also grow and develop and bear good seed. For instance, in the bible the illustration of *the parable of the sower,* the seed represents the Word of God. If we allow the Word of God to *germinate,* which is to sprout or develop, and *permeate,* which is to saturate, every detail of our lives, then the seed principle used as the Word of God will only result in producing and bringing forth good fruit in our lives. However, it is very important not to miss that the development of the seed is determined by the quality of the soil in which the seed is planted. We need to provide God's seed with good soil like that in the parable of the sower (Luke 8:5-15). As Christians, we allow the seed to fall on good and fertile ground by hearing the word, retaining it and persevering.

In summary, our hearts follow what is truly dear to us. We can look at where we spend our money, energy and time and see where our priorities lie. Let us make sure we examine our hearts daily, so that we can constantly be aware of where it is. Also, if we sense that something unwholesome is creeping into our hearts, guard our hearts. *"Above all else, guard your heart, for it is the wellspring of life"* (Proverbs 4:23).

Finally, invest in the things of the Kingdom. The more time we spend with God, the more our hearts will value the things that God values. Consequently, my brothers and sisters, the desires of our hearts shall be granted. *"Dear friends, if our hearts do not condemn us, we have confidence before God, and receive from him anything we ask, because we obey his commands and do what pleases him"* (I John 3:21-22).

ATTITUDE

For the word of God is living and active. Sharper than any double-edged sword, it penetrates even to dividing soul and spirit, joints and marrow; it judges the thoughts and attitudes of the heart.
(Hebrews 4:12)

Could it be that our attitudes are a hindrance to our blessings? Our outward attitudes are just a manifestation of what is going on in our hearts. It has been said that our eyes are a window into our souls, and the bible tells us that our attitudes are a window into our hearts. This subject of the attitude of the heart that Hebrews 4:12 talks about is so important, for a lot of people feel that their blessings or lack of blessings derive from their actions or deeds. However, we will actually give an account based on what is in our hearts as well, because the bible teaches us that man looks at the outer appearances, but God looks at the heart. Hebrews 4:13 also teaches us that nothing is hidden from God's sight in all creation. Everything is uncovered and laid bare before the eyes of Him to whom we must give account.

Our attitudes have far reaching effects that can prove to be a fountain for both constructive and destructive behavior in our lives. Interestingly, research shows that bad or negative attitudes rarely stem from exposure to bad or negative life situations, but rather, bad or negative attitudes almost always stem from how a person perceives or responds to the negative circumstances. That is why people can experience similar circumstances and come away with totally different mindsets about the situation. Martha Washington says it best, *"The greater our happiness or misery depends upon our dispositions and not our circumstances."*

This subject about attitudes is so important, for it is the driving force for so many people's actions, and if we are not extremely careful to watch our attitudes, we can be headed for disaster. If we are totally honest with ourselves, we get into the most trouble when our attitudes conflict with the attitude of Christ. The only way to overcome the battle with our bad attitudes is to overcome the battle that starts in our minds.

In order for us to overcome certain strongholds and battles we have ruminating in our minds, our attitudes must be the same as Christ Jesus (Philippians 2:5). Subsequently, we must also learn to take captive every thought to make it obedient to Christ (2 Corinthians 10:5b.) Also, we must let the Word of God penetrate even dividing soul and spirit, joints and marrow and allow the Word of God to judge the thoughts and attitudes of our hearts (Hebrews 4:12b). As humans, we are incapable of judging our own hearts ourselves because our hearts will deceive us, but the Word of God is living and active and knows how to penetrate right down to the truth.

Fortunately, God does not just tell us to have the mind of Christ without teaching us and giving us many examples in His Word on how to make new the attitude of our minds (Ephesians 4:23). It is important to note that God's Word also teaches us that the spirit and the flesh are in direct competition with each other. So in order not to give way to our flesh, we must understand that we are in a spiritual battle that can only be fought by spiritual weapons. Gratefully, greater is He that is in us than he that is in the world. Thus, as Christians, we are more than conquerors through Christ which strengthens us. The bible teaches us that it is the Spirit who gives life; the flesh profits nothing. We want to make sure that we are being led not by our flesh but rather led by the Spirit.

As humans we all have our own individual personalities. Our personality traits come from both hereditary factors, meaning we come out of the womb with a certain personality, as well as environmental factors which help shape our personality. Whichever the case, God has uniquely and wonderfully shaped our personalities to be what He desires in order to accomplish His perfect will through us. However, even though God uses our individual uniqueness to carry out His will, God does require from us uniformity in personality as it relates to us exhibiting the *Fruit of the Spirit*. In other words, our unique personalities should never trump the personality of Christ, which is in essence, the *Fruit of the Spirit* which we should all strive to possess as Christians.

Galatians 5:22 tells us precisely how we are to walk/live by the Spirit

1) We are to exhibit *Love*

The longer we live, we come to realize that people in general do not always give us the motivation or inspiration to love. Unfortunately, oftentimes people will diminish your motivation to love if you let them. Moreover, if were not watchful, we can put so many conditions on our love that it would be virtually impossible to meet. However, there is no way around it - choosing not to love someone means we are out of God's perfect will for our lives. Gilbert K. Chesterton stated this fact clearly: *"Love means to love that which is unlovable; or it is no virtue at all."* In other words, Matthew 5:46-47 tells us that, *"If you love those who love you, what reward will you get? Are not even the tax collectors doing that? And if you greet only your own people, what are you doing more than others? Do not even pagans do that?"*

It is through our love that differentiates Christians from unbelievers. As mature Christians, we work towards not needing love always demonstrated to us in order to give love. In the nature of life, there may be times when we demonstrate love that we may not receive it back (at least not from that same person). Oftentimes, it is the people that act unlovable that need love the most. You might be asking the question, *"how are we supposed to love someone who is not deserving of our love at all?"* Loving someone unconditionally will never come from our feeble fleshly attempts. In fact, God knows as humans, relying on our moods and emotions is senseless, for they are moving targets and our hearts only deceive us. The bible says, *"He who trusts in his own heart is a fool, but he who walks wisely will be delivered."* We have to depend on an unchanging God that thought it not robbery to first love us in spite of ourselves, even though we don't deserve His love. Also, recognizing if we are honest with ourselves, we are not always lovable either. Consequently, when others recognize this endearing quality of love in us and wonder how are we able to love so unconditionally we can tell them that God is the reason we love. Our love comes from Him and the help of the Holy Spirit.

2) We are to exhibit *Joy*

When it comes to real joy, we must look at our individual circumstances through the eyes of God. Nothing will kill, steal and destroy our joy more, than looking at the world's standard of happiness whether it is watching certain television shows, trying to keep up with our neighbors (joneses) or comparing our lives with our Facebook *"friends"*. The bible speaks of it, and there have been countless secular studies that show that joy, unspeakable joy does not come from things or circumstances but an attitude of gratitude. Abraham Lincoln said a profound statement, *"We can complain because rose bushes have thorns, or rejoice because thorn bushes have roses."* Dale Carnegie says, *"It isn't what you have or who you are or where you are or what you are doing that makes you happy or unhappy. It is what you think about."* This is why guarding our minds is paramount. We have to protect our thoughts as if our very lives depended on it. True happiness is to enjoy the present without anxious dependence upon the future, not to amuse ourselves with either hopes or fears, but to rest satisfied with what we have. This is sufficient, for he that is so wants nothing. The greatest blessings of mankind are within us and within our reach. As Seneca stated, *"A wise man is content with his lot, whatever it may be, without wishing for what he has not."*

3) We are to exhibit *Peace*

Peace is a concept that most people desperately desire to have but struggle with how to acquire. In general, people do not lack having peace for a lack of trying to obtain it. In fact, there are various ways people go about acquiring peace. Unfortunately, some of these ways can be destructive, unhealthy, expensive and downright unsuccessful. *"In whom the god of this world hath blinded the minds of them which believe not, lest the light of the glorious gospel of Christ, who is the image of God, should shine unto them"* (2 Corinthians 4:4).

Make no mistake about it - the devil is the god of this world. Therefore, the spiritual Fruit of the Spirit

Peace, which is a gift from God that is available to all believers, will not and cannot come from the things of this world, but only from God. *"I have said these things to you, that in me you may have peace. In the world you will have tribulation. But take heart; I have overcome the world,"* (John 16:33). However, greater is He who is in us than he that is in the world. God is not only greater than he that's in the world but God has *All* power in His hands. So no matter what our situation is God has already promised us peace that is sufficient for any situation as long as we keep our minds stayed on Him.

"You cannot find peace by avoiding life," Virginia Woolf. Some people think they can insure having peace by abstaining from the game of life. However, godly peace is not the absence of trouble, but a divine tranquilizer in the midst of trouble, danger and sorrow. Augustine of Hippo said it best, *"Thou hast made us for thyself, O Lord, and our heart is restless until it finds its rest in thee."*

4) We are to exhibit *Patience*

Patience makes us wise. Patience allows people to be human around you. The bible teaches an overarching theme that a person without patience is a person without wisdom. In order to guard our attitude of patience we have to combat the enemy of patience which is anger. Anger and patience are usually direct opposites of each other. In order to defeat anger, it is important to know why and where from the root of most anger comes. James 4:1-2a gives us some insight, *"What causes fights and quarrels among you? Don't they come from your desires that battle within you? You want something but you don't get it."*

When we find ourselves having a problem with a bad temper or were easily angered by what others say and do, we are enslaved by our own emotions. Our emotions derive from our thinking. If we continue to ignite negative thought patterns in our minds about ourselves and others, there are bound to be serious unhealthy consequences.

Research has shown that people who cannot control their anger end up alienating people who are in their lives. Also, people who cannot control their anger often times end up with bad nerves, insurmountable levels of stress, upset stomachs, problems with sleeping as well as various illnesses. Unfortunately, not only does the person dealing with uncontrolled anger experience these symptoms, but research also shows that the spouses and children exhibit these symptoms as well. To get angry is not a sin, but to act ungodly because of anger is. Ephesians 4:26 says, *"Be angry and sin not."*

5) We are to exhibit *Kindness*

It has been said that without kindness, no act can truly be done in love. According to Oxford American Dictionary, kindness is *"when a person has genuine concern and care for others and shows this by being compassionate and considerate"*. Kindness is like a boomerang - the more you give, the more you get back. God's Word says it this way, *you reap what you sow*. Joseph Joubert agrees, saying that *"kindness is loving people more than they deserve"*. Kindness is a gift we give people that resonates with them long after they have left. On the contrary, the opposite is also true. People remember the feelings of unkindness shown to them long after they have left us as well.

Consider the following illustration by KiranKumar Roy:

> One day, a poor boy who was selling goods from door to door to pay his way through school, found he had only one thin dime left, and he was hungry. He decided he would ask for a meal at the next house. However, he lost his nerve when a lovely young woman opened the door. Instead of a meal he asked for a drink of water.
>
> She thought he looked hungry so brought him a large glass of milk. He drank it slowly, and then asked the young woman, "How much do I owe you?"
>
> "You don't owe me anything," she replied.

"Mother has taught us never to accept any pay for an act of kindness."

He said, "Then I thank you from my heart." As the boy, whose name was Howard Kelly, left that house, he not only felt stronger physically, but his faith in God and man was strong also. He had been ready to give up and quit.

Years later that young woman became critically ill. The local doctors were baffled. They finally sent her to the big city, where they called in specialists to study her rare disease. Dr. Howard Kelly was called in for the consultation. When he heard the name of the town she came from, a strange light filled his eyes. Immediately he rose and went down the hall of the hospital to find the woman's room.

Dressed in his doctor's gown he went in to see her. He recognized her at once. He went back to the consultation room determined to do his best to save her life. From that day he gave special attention to the case.

After a long struggle, the battle was won. Dr. Kelly requested the business office to pass the final bill to him for approval.

He looked at it, then wrote something on the edge and the bill was sent to her room. She feared to open it, for she was sure it would take the rest of her life to pay for it all. Finally she looked, and something caught her attention on the side of the bill. She cried when she read these words.....

"Paid in full with one glass of milk"

6) We are to exhibit *Goodness*

Goodness is the desire to be a blessing to others by carrying out good deeds motivated by righteousness. Ephesians chapters 4 and 5 give specific ways goodness is to be expressed in our lives. Some of these are, speaking truthfully, not sinning in our anger, not stealing but doing something "useful". We are not to do hurtful, harmful things but helpful, beneficial, useful things. Then, we are to build up one another with our conversation. We must get rid of all malice and be kind, compassionate, forgiving, imitators of God and Christ, living lives of love. In this way we align ourselves with the Holy Spirit and avoid grieving Him.

7) We are to exhibit *Faithfulness*

Having the attitude of faith means we believe God for the things we hope for, even though we do not see the evidence (Hebrews 11:1). Faith is the confidence we have in God; that He will work in our lives and on our behalf, for our good and for His glory. It is important that we do not put our faith in inanimate objects, such as, prayer cloths, holy water or the like. Also, we have to be careful not to place our faith in other people, or even ourselves, for time will reveal that misplaced faith will ultimately fail us.

In addition, it is important to recognize that faith is not anti-intellectual. God's Word can and has always been able to stand the test of time. God gave us our intellect and reason abilities, and does not want them to be mutually exclusive, but in fact, mutually complimentary. God wants us to use our intellect through His Spirit to have better understanding of His Word. "*As for these four youths, God gave them knowledge and intelligence in every branch of literature and wisdom; Daniel even understood all kinds of visions and dreams"* (Daniel 1:17 NASB).

Moreover, faith is not a self-help positive thoughts motivational seminar with relaxing breathing techniques. Thinking positive and deep breaths will not hurt you, but it is not faith. It is in a sovereign God alone, who we should put our faith and confidence in.

8) We are to exhibit *Gentleness*

It has been said by Steven Kendrick and Alex Kendrick that *"Some people are like lemons: when life squeezes them, they pour out a sour response. Some are more like peaches: when the pressure is on, the result is still sweet."* Ungratefulness, bitterness and pride can cause any of us to act sour and not gentle. In fact, people who are easily irritable are locked, loaded and ready to overreact. It is only when we allow God's love to overpower our hearts that we become a calmer and gentler Spirit.

Gentleness is restraint and strength at the same time. Donald Gee gives this illustration:

> There was a guide that was taking a group of visitors through a factory. One of the things he showed them was a giant steam hammer capable of flattening an automobile. Then the guide put down a walnut and had the hammer break the shell without hurting the meat of the nut.

What an illustration of gentleness as power under perfect control!

9) We are to exhibit *Self-control*

I would venture to say that this topic of self-control is one of the most important aspects of a Christian's life. There are many areas in our lives that we must learn to control if we want to walk in victory; however, one area which should be at the top of the list is controlling our emotions. For some of us we have allowed our emotions to become pilot in our lives, and God's Word is relegated to co-pilot or the back seat. Our emotions can be the driving force behind our thoughts and even our actions if were not careful, and what a scary place to be! When we are driven by our emotions and not on the truth, which is the Word of God, we set ourselves up for disaster.

Often times the devil whispers to us accusing accusations about ourselves and others, distorts the truth or flat out lies about circumstances, influencing us to feel shame and causing us to be unfairly critical of others. *"God's word is a lamp unto my feet and a light unto my path,"* (Psalm 119:105).

Let us be careful to take heed to everything that is in God's Word, for His word is protection for us, even when it means overriding our emotions.

4

REVERENCE

Oh, that their hearts would be inclined to fear me and keep all my commands always, so that it might go well with them and their children forever! (Deuteronomy 5:29)

Blessed is the man who fears the Lord (Psalm 112:1)

Fear and reverence of the Lord goes hand in hand. In fact, the bible uses the word fear as it relates to reverencing the Lord countless times. For example, in Exodus 1:17 the bible says, *"The midwives, however, feared God and did not do what the king of Egypt had told them to do; they let the boys live."* In addition, Exodus 18:21 says, *"But select capable men from all the people – men who fear God, trustworthy men who hate dishonest gain."*

Leviticus 19 explains to us that even when we do good deeds, it is out of our fear and reverence to the Lord. Leviticus 19:14 records the following, *"Do not curse the deaf or put a stumbling block in front of the blind, but fear your God."* Leviticus 19:32 puts it this way, *"Rise in the presence of the aged, show respect for the elderly and revere your God."* Also, Pharaoh and his officials did not *fear* the Lord, so consequently, a significant portion of their livelihood in the form of flax and barley were destroyed.

It is apparent from these passages that when we fear the Lord, it keeps us from submitting to our own sinful nature. On the contrary, when we do not reverence the Lord, it can keep us from our blessings.

Conditions and requirements of a believer in order to receive God's promises:

To show reverence for God means to humble yourself (Jeremiah 44:10)

The world sees humility and being humble as a

weakness, while God sees us being humble as a gateway for being blessed. I Peter 5:6-7 says, *"Humble yourselves, therefore, under the mighty hand of God so that at the proper time He may exalt you, casting all your anxieties on Him, because He cares for you."* God delights in blessing and exalting us, especially when we show humility towards Him. One of the reasons God desires for us to humble ourselves before Him is because He knows that it is then that we fully surrender our wills to Him, and trust and believe that He, alone, is our provider. Jesus is our ultimate example of being humble to our heavenly Father. Philippians 2:8-11 says, *"And being found in human form, He humbled Himself by becoming obedient to the point of death, even death on a cross. Therefore God has highly exalted Him and bestowed on Him the name that is above every name, so that at the name of Jesus every knee should bow, in heaven and on earth and under the earth, and every tongue confess that Jesus Christ is Lord, to the glory of God the Father."*

II Corinthians 7:1 – To show reverence for God

perfects holiness

The closer we get to God, the clearer we see the difference between our imperfections and God's true perfect holiness. The bible illustrates many examples of how people felt when they entered into God's presence. First, when Isaiah saw the glory of the Lord, he said," *Woe is me! For I am undone; because I am a man of unclean lips, and I dwell in the midst of a people of unclean lips: for mine eyes have seen the King, the LORD of hosts.*" Also, when Job compared himself to the glory and holiness of God, he said in Job 42:5-6, "*I have heard of thee by the hearing of the ear: but now mine eye seeth thee. Wherefore I abhor myself, and repent in dust and ashes.*"

God knows that, as humans, we are imperfect. However, God is so worthy to be honored and revered! To reverence God means to be in complete awe, with undeniable humility towards Him. Let us read this passage that John saw in his vision of the Lord as if we were reading it for the first time.

(Revelation 4:2-11) *And immediately I was in the spirit: and, behold, a throne was set in heaven, and one sat on the throne. And he that sat was to look upon like a jasper and a sardine stone: and there was a rainbow round about the throne, in sight like unto an emerald. And round about the throne were four and twenty seats: and upon the seats I saw four and twenty elders sitting, clothed in white raiment; and they had on their heads crowns of gold. And out of the throne proceeded lightnings and thunderings and voices: and there were seven lamps of fire burning before the throne, which are the seven Spirits of God. And before the throne there was a sea of glass like unto crystal: and in the midst of the throne, and round about the throne, were four beasts full of eyes before and behind. And the first beast was like a lion, and the second beast like a calf, and the third beast had a face as a man, and the fourth beast was like a flying eagle. And the four beasts had each of them six wings about him; and they were full of eyes within: and they rest not day and night, saying, Holy, Holy, Holy, LORD God Almighty, which was, and is, and is to come. And when those beasts give glory and honour and thanks to him that sat on the throne, who liveth for ever and ever, the four and twenty elders fall down before him that sat on the throne, and worship him that liveth for ever and ever, and cast their crowns before the throne, saying, Thou art worthy, O Lord, to receive glory and honour and power: for thou hast created all things, and for thy pleasure they are and were created."*

When John saw the glory and majesty of the Lord he said in Revelation 1:17, *"And when I saw him, I fell at his feet as dead. And he laid his right hand upon me, saying unto me, Fear not; I am the first and the last."* Oh, let us always reverence and behold our God! Just like II Corinthians 7:1 says, *"Let us purify ourselves from everything that contaminates body and spirit, perfecting holiness out of reverence for God."*

Ephesians 5:21 – To show reverence for God means to submit to one another

A true test of our reverencing God means we are also humble to our fellow man. The bible teaches us that the two greatest commandments in the law are these:

1). *"Love the Lord your God with all your heart and with all your soul and with all your mind."*

2). *"And the second is like it: 'Love your neighbor as yourself.'"*

We love our neighbors by submitting to one another. We

can submit to one another by serving each other when we see a need, by being patient with one another, by edifying one another with our mouths and building each other up as opposed to tearing them down, by forgiving one another, and by loving one another with agape love (love not based on our feelings but based on God's love for us).

Hebrews 12:28 – To show reverence for God means to worship God with reverence and awe

The bible teaches us that we are to worship God in Spirit and in Truth. The bible also tells us *"not to give up meeting together, as some are in the habit of doing, but let us encourage one another- and all the more as you see the Day approaching* (Hebrews 10:25).

The bible instructs us to be in relationship with other believers because this is where we learn to serve, practice forgiveness and grow up in the faith. Romans 12:5 says, *"…so in Christ we who are many form one body, and each member belongs to all the others." The body is a unit, though it is made up of many parts; and though its parts are many, they form one body. So it is with Christ,"* (1 Corinthians 12:12).

Colossians 3:22-24 – To show reverence for God means to work unto the Lord and not unto man

As Christians we have to fight the temptation of needing adoration from man for anything. We tread on rocky ground when we do things to be seen or praised. Galatians 1:10 says, *"Am I now trying to win the approval of human beings, or of God? Or am I trying to please people? If I were still trying to please people, I would not be a servant of Christ."* Although it is true that it would be nice to be shown appreciation for the good deeds we do, make no mistake about it, God sees everything. Not only does He see the bad we do, He also sees the good we do. For every unselfish act we exhibit; for every blood, sweat and tears we put forth to help someone; for every undeserving grace we give to someone; for every painstaking effort we put in at work; for every spiritual reasonable service we do for God's kingdom; for every decision we make to show the Fruit of the Spirit and not our fleshly nature all because we want to glorify God, God sees!

Yes, we will not always get acclamation from man or women for our efforts; however, there are definite rewards given to us every time we decide to work unto the Lord. "*So when you give to the needy, do not announce it with trumpets, as the hypocrites do in the synagogues and on the streets, to be honored by others. Truly I tell you, they have received their reward in full. But when you give to the needy, do not let your left hand know what your right hand is doing, so that your giving may be in secret. Then your Father, who sees what is done in secret, will reward you,*" (Matthew 6:2-4). And Paul puts it this way, "*Remember this: Whoever sows sparingly will also reap sparingly, and whoever sows generously will also reap generously,*" (II Corinthians 9:6).

I Peter 3:2 – When women show purity and reverence their inner beauty shines forth

I Peter 3:3-4 says, *"Do not let your adorning be external—the braiding of hair and the putting on of gold jewelry, or the clothing you wear— but let your adorning be the hidden person of the heart with the imperishable beauty of a gentle and quiet spirit, which in God's sight is very precious."* This verse is surely not suggesting that women cannot go to the hairdresser, or that women should just physically let themselves go. However, this scripture is saying that putting forth all our efforts in adorning the outside and not working on our inner beauty is futile. The only way to exhibit real beauty is to exhibit the Fruit of the Spirit. The Fruit of the Spirit enables us to forgo undesirable traits that shine on us like a spotlight and make us look spiritually ugly. Some of these traits include hatred, jealousy, greed, impatience, irreverence to God or man, gossiping, bitterness and the like.

Bitterness, specifically, is like a wildfire that can utterly destroy a soul. Here are some very poignant quotes pertaining to bitterness:

- Growth in wisdom may be exactly measured by decrease in bitterness - Friedrich Nietzsche
- Bitterness imprisons life; love releases it - Harry Emerson Fosdick
- When our hatred is too bitter it places us below those whom we hate. – FranCois De La Rochefoucauld
- One may have been a fool, but there's no foolishness like being bitter. - Kathleen Norris
- It is a simple but sometimes forgotten truth that the greatest enemy to present joy and high hopes is the cultivation of retrospective bitterness. - Robert G. Menzies
- Part of the problem with the word 'disabilities' is that it immediately suggests an inability to see, or hear, or walk, or do other things that many of us take for granted. But, what of people who cannot *feel*? Or *talk* about their feelings? Or *manage* their feelings in constructive ways? What of people who are not able to form close and strong relationships? Or people who cannot find fulfillment in their lives? Or those who have lost hope, who live in disappointment and bitterness and find in life no joy, no love? These, it seems to me, are the real "disabilities." – Fred Rogers

Let us continue to work on our inner beauty by meditating on God's Word daily and asking God to fill us with His Holy Spirit.

Promises and blessings that God gives us as believers when we reverence Him

1) That it will keep you from sin.

> *Moses said to the people, "Do not be afraid. God has come to test you, so that the fear of God will be with you to keep you from sinning,"* (Exodus 20:20)

2) That it will go well with you

> *Oh, that their hearts would be inclined to fear me and keep all my commands always, so that it might go well with them and their children forever!* (Deuteronomy 5:29)

3) That you may enjoy long life

> *So that you, your children and their children after them may fear the LORD your God as long as you live by keeping all his decrees and commands that I give you, and so that you may enjoy long life* (Deuteronomy 6:2).

4) That you will always prosper

> *The LORD commanded us to obey all these decrees and to fear the LORD our God, so that we might always prosper and be kept alive, as is the case today,* (Deuteronomy 6:24)

5) That you will demonstrate God's power

> *He did this so that all the peoples of the earth might know that the hand of the LORD is powerful and so that you might always fear the LORD your God,* (Joshua 4:24)

6) That the Lord will entrust you with leadership

> *I put in charge of Jerusalem my brother Hanani, along with Hananiah the commander of the citadel, because he was a man of integrity and feared God more than most people do,* (Nehemiah 7:2)

7) That the Lord will give you instruction

> *Who, then, are those who fear the LORD? He will instruct them in the ways they should choose,* (Psalm 25:12)

8) That the Lord will confide in you

> *The LORD confides in those who fear him; he makes his covenant known to them,* (Psalm 25:14)

9) That you will not fear man

The LORD is my light and my salvation, whom shall I fear? The LORD is the stronghold of my life of whom shall I be afraid?, (Psalm 27:1)

10) That you will lack nothing

Fear the LORD, you his holy people, for those who fear him lack nothing, (Psalm 34:9)

11) That you will be blessed with wealthy honor and life.

Humility is the fear of the LORD; its wages are riches and honor and life, (Proverbs 22:4)

ACTIONS

I the Lord search the heart and examine the mind, to reward a man according to his conduct, according to what his deeds deserve. (Jeremiah 17:10)

Jesus Christ said by their fruit you shall know them, not by their disclaimers. - William S. Burroughs

It has been noted that actions speak louder than words. Truth is, I have found that during many situations in life, words are just noise... and actions are the ONLY things that speak. - Steve Maraboli

---

"Indifference: It takes 43 muscles to frown and 17 to smile, but it doesn't take any to just sit there with a dumb look on your face," (Source www.despair.com). This quote may be funny, however, God never intended on His children to live a life of indifference. On the contrary, if anyone is to live purposeful lives and make a difference in the world, it would be Christians. Once you become a Christian, one of your daily concerns is how you can please God with your living. However, with God, no one could ever be pleasing to Him based on performance. God's standard is perfection, and no goodness on our part can ever compensate for our sins. We may please man with our actions, but "*all have sinned, and come short of the glory of God,*" (Romans 3:23).

Only the precious blood of Jesus can make us righteous and put us in good standing with God. However, because of God's insurmountable goodness and mercy toward us, and the sacrificing of His Son Jesus on our behalf on the cross, we want to show our thanks to Him - by our faith and trust in Him, as well as our actions. As explained by Steve Maraboli, "*While intent is the seed of manifestation, action is the water that nourishes the seed. Your actions must reflect your goals in order to achieve true success.*"

There are three characteristics of action that are especially pleasing to God

1) Discipline

Self-discipline is that which, next to virtue, truly and essentially raises one man above another - Joseph Addison.

According to the Oxford American Desk Dictionary, one definition of discipline means "to have controlled behavior, persistence and obedience resulting from such training". There are many examples of people in the bible who fulfilled their purpose and accomplished God's call on their lives. Overwhelmingly, Daniel was a perfect example of how fulfilling our purpose in life is directly connected to exhibiting the essential characteristic of discipline. Though Daniel did not object to the schooling nor the name change (Belteshazzar) that the Babylonian regime gave him, he did, however, reject and had the discipline to refrain from the kings rich food. Some scholars suggest this refusal to eat the king's meat was so important to Daniel because, in his early education before he went into captivity into Babylon, he learned about Proverbs 23: 1-3, which states, *"When you sit to dine with a ruler, note well what is before you, and put a knife to your throat if you are given to gluttony. Do not crave his delicacies, for that food is deceptive."*

I surmise that Daniel saw the dangers in indulging without using discretion, and wanted to always stay alert and stay vigilant, in order to glorify the One, True God. Additionally, it was the practice of dying to self and refusing moral compromise that gave Daniel the mental and spiritual discipline he needed for future tests. Furthermore, Daniel realized that rejecting the world's way of doing things helped him stay focused on the spiritual matters of fulfilling his calling.

In addition to the example of Daniel, there are many other illustrations in the bible, as well as in our everyday lives, where we see the act of discipline serving well in people's lives. As Christians, there are countless of ways we can also show discipline such as: 1) when were tempted to do wrong we choose right; 2) when were tempted to be stingy we give; 3) when were tempted to hate we love; 4) when were tempted to complain we give thanks; 5) when were tempted to overindulge we refrain; 6) when were tempted to give up we keep pressing on; 7) when were tempted to be self-centered we become others centered. Thomas Fuller said it best, "Serving one's own passions is the greatest slavery."

Brian Tracy, author of the book The Power of Discipline, illustrates this as he talks about an experience he had:

> A legend in the field of success and achievement, Kop Kopmeyer had written four large books, each of which contained 250 success principles that he had derived from more than fifty years of research and study. I had read all four books from cover to cover, more than once.
>
> After we had chatted for a while, I asked him the question that many people in this situation

would ask, "Of all the one thousand success principles that you have discovered, which do you think is the most important?"

He smiled at me with a twinkle in his eye, as if he had been asked this question many times, and replied, without hesitating, "The most important success principle of all was stated by Thomas Huxley many years ago. He said, "Do what you should do, when you should do it, whether you feel like it or not."

He continues,

There are 999 other success principles that I have found in my reading and experience, but without discipline, none of them work.

2) Development of Good Habits

We have to be aware of our every thought process as well as our actions, for our actions soon become our habits. One bad habit can throw us off course from experiencing all of our blessings. *Habit, if not resisted, soon becomes necessity*, (St. Augustine).

A habit is an act we repeatedly do usually involuntarily. Charles Noble says, "First we make our habits, then our habits make us." That is why habits are so powerful because they can work for us or against us. There are obviously some good habits people form as well as some bad habits.

One bad habit that God does not want us to develop is the mindset of mediocrity. Oxford American Dictionary states mediocre as, "of only average or fairly low quality." "Indifferent, unexceptional, run of the mill, lacking originality." This term exemplifies anything but Christian ideology, because we know that God formed us all to be exceptional and original, to do extraordinary things according to God's divine purpose for us, to the glory of God.

Another common bad habit many people find hard to shake is the ability to control negative thinking. Psychologist Hara Estroff Marano, author of an article in the journal, *Psychology Today*, talks about how negative thinking patterns can seep into the brain so automatically that it becomes a habit and no longer feels like a choice. She goes on to say that negative thinking is one of the strongest habit patterns.

All is not lost, Marano adds: *"You may not always be able to control how you feel but you can control how you think."* She goes on to say that it is very possible to control what you think but you have to change the quality of your thoughts from negative to positive on purpose. Human Beings on an average think between 25,000 - 50,000 thoughts per day. Many of those thoughts are negative. We have to learn how to flip the switch. When we start thinking negatively, we have to quickly discard the negative thoughts, and change them to positive thoughts.

In addition, when we change the way we think, then we will change the way we feel. In other words, as II Corinthians 10:5 so eloquently states, *"We demolish arguments and every pretension that sets itself up against the knowledge of God, and we take captive every thought to make it obedient to Christ."* When we forfeit the mind of Christ, and we choose to dwell on the negative instead of the positive, we lose our joy and our peace. Additionally, *"If you don't watch out, putting on your unhappiness in the morning can become as instinctive as putting on your clothes,"* (Robert Brault).

Furthermore, laziness is another bad habit some people deal with. *"The man who waits for roast duck to fly into mouth must wait very, very long time,* (Chinese proverb). Solomon understood this fact as well: *"I passed by the field of a sluggard, by the vineyard of a man lacking sense, and behold, it was all overgrown with thorns; the ground was covered with nettles, and its stone wall was broken down. Then I saw and considered it; I looked and received instruction. A little sleep, a little slumber, a little folding of the hands to rest, and poverty will come upon you like a robber, and want like an armed man,"* (Proverbs 24:30-

34). As Anne Frank put it, *"Laziness may appear attractive but work gives satisfaction."*

Oftentimes, we think people are lazy just because they lack the desire to work hard; however, research shows there are a lot of reasons people have developed the bad habit of laziness. Sometimes people are lazy because fear has paralyzed and immobilized them so much so that they are stuck in a rut. At other times, some people are indecisive and have a hard time making a decision. Author Winkie Pratney quotes, *"Many say they can't get God's guidance, when they really mean they wish He would show them an easier way."*

Still other times people are perfectionists, and have a hard time finishing anything for fear of failure. *"A man would do nothing if he waited until he could do it so well that no one could find fault,"* (John Henry Newman). Some people have a low level of confidence and cannot picture themselves being successful at anything. Others, because of a lack of knowledge or feeling of inadequacy, shy away from doing what is needed to be done. Some people feel the task at hand seem too big and insurmountable, and they do not know how to break them into smaller tasks. And yet, for others, their faith is not strong enough to do what God has ordained for them to do.

Nonetheless, whatever the reason, let us ask God to help us identify any areas of laziness that might be in our lives. Let us allow God to renew our minds and help us to overcome this bad habit so we can move forward into our promise lands. "*Do not throw away your confidence; it will be richly rewarded. You need to persevere so that when you have done the will of God, you will receive what he has promised,*" (Hebrews 10:35–36).

Additionally, Emory Horvath talks about how we can conquer *ungodly* habits. He says,

> Getting strong on the inside will help you throw off bad habits on the outside. Matthew

12:29 says, "*Or else how can one enter into a strong man's house, and spoil his goods, except he first bind the strong man? And then he will spoil his house.*"

Horvath continues to say,

> In order to bind a man, you are going to have to be the stronger one. You have to be stronger than the strong man. You have to get stronger on the inside than the habit on the outside. It's like colds and your immune system. Some try to get rid of a cold by taking cold medications. But if your immune system is weak, the cold will just come right back on you. It's better to strengthen the immune system and then throw it off. In order to throw a habit, you are going to have to get stronger than the thing which is pulling you down. If you're not strong in God, if you do not have the Word strongly in you, any progress you make will only be temporary.

Practice yourself, for heaven's sake in little things, and then proceed to greater

Developing good habits usually manifest itself in our doing good deeds. (Epictetus)

Doing the smallest gesture of good for someone often has a big impact. Edwin Chapin says, *"Every action of our lives touches on some chord that will vibrate in eternity."* Every single Christian has been called and ordained to be a blessing to someone in some way, and glorify God in the process. If you do not think you have anything to offer, think about this, *"If you think you're too small to have an impact, try going to bed with a mosquito in the room,"* (Anita Roddick). *"May God make you complete in every good work to do His will, working in you what is well pleasing in His sight, through Jesus Christ, to whom be glory forever and ever. Amen"* (Hebrews 13:21).

3) The ability to die to self

> "And he said to all, "If anyone would come after me, let him deny himself and take up his cross daily and follow me. For whoever would save his life will lose it, but whoever loses his life for my sake will save it." (Luke 9:23-24).

This bible verse is yet again another example of how God's ways are higher than our ways, and the way

God operates is different from the way the world functions. According to this verse, when we deny ourselves, we are essentially dying to our flesh. We are surrendering our will to our Father, just like Jesus surrendered His will to His Father, by praying, *"Yet not my will, but yours be done,"* (Luke 22:42b).

This is why, as Christians, we have to understand that our unfulfilled desires will never be met by the world's antics. We live in this world, but we are not of this world. *"Do not love the world or anything in the world. If anyone loves the world, love for the Father is not in them. For everything in the world—the lust of the flesh, the lust of the eyes, and the pride of life—comes not from the Father but from the world. The world and its desires pass away, but whoever does the will of God lives forever,"* (I John 2:15-17).

As we grow as Christians, and we start to hate the things that God hates and love the things that God loves, our old nature has to die. This transformation in us does not always come naturally, easily or quickly. In fact, Paul talks about in Romans 7 the agonizing realizations Christians deal with as it relates to our flesh. Those things we despise, we find ourselves doing. Those things we desire we fail to accomplish. Paul agrees with the law and wants to do what is right, but his body does not always respond accordingly. Romans 7:15-20 says, *"I do not understand what I do. For what I want to do I do not do, but what I hate I do. And if I do what I do not want to do, I agree that the law is good. As it is, it is no longer I myself who do it, but it is sin living in me. For I know that good itself does not dwell in me, that is, in my sinful nature. For I have the desire to do what is good, but I cannot carry it out. For I do not do the good I want to do, but the evil I do not want to do—this I keep on doing. Now if I do what I do not want to do, it is no longer I who do it, but it is sin living in me that does it."*

Paul is not alone - we all get frustrated with the weakness of our fleshly bodies. Things may sound hopeless for us, but thanks to God it is not hopeless for us. God exposes our fleshly weakness so we will be receptive to His spiritual solution. No man would understand our sinning against the law, except through divine illumination. Due to the fall of Adam and Eve, we were born into sin, and did not have the ability to live righteously in our own strength. However, due to Jesus dying on the cross for our sins, we have victory over sin in Christ!

Jack Wellman, author of *The Christian Crier*, puts it like this:

> "Although we still stumble and fall, we get back up. That's the difference between an unsaved person and a saved person; the unsaved person doesn't fall into sin, they dive into it with pleasure and swim in it with no desire to get out of it…but the saved person has become *"a new creature in Christ"* (II Corinthians 5:17) and although they are not sinless, they do want to sin less!
>
> Every Christian falls and stumbles but they get back up, dust themselves off, and keep moving forward, growing in holiness by the help of God's Spirit. *"The old has passed away; behold, the new has come"* (II Corinthians 5:17b), but we also realize that *"All this is from God"* (II Corinthian 5:18a)."

During the Civil War, an unknown soldier was quoted saying the following about this issue:

> I asked God for strength that I might achieve. I was made weak that I might learn humbly to obey. I asked God for health that I might do greater things. I was given infirmity that I might do better things. I asked for riches that I might be happy. I was given poverty that I might be wise. I asked for power that I might have the praise of men. I was given weakness that I might feel the need of God. I asked for all things that I might enjoy life. I was given life that I might enjoy all things. I got nothing that I asked for – but everything I had hoped for…
>
> Almost despite myself, my unspoken prayers were answered. I am among all men most richly blessed."

This has been confirmed by Galatians 2:20:

I have been crucified with Christ and I no longer live, but Christ lives in me. The life I now live in the body, I live by faith in the Son of God, who loved me and gave himself for me."

APRIL SCHELL BLACK

COURAGE

When they saw the courage of Peter and John and realized that they were unschooled, ordinary men, they were astonished and they took note that the men had been with Jesus. (Acts 4:13)

The only reason we can have courage in a world with so much uncertainty, danger and wickedness, is because our heavenly Father is with us! The Lord knows and understands our inherent fears; however, He spoke these reassuring words for us:

> *"Therefore I say to you, do not worry about your life, what you will eat or what you will drink; nor about your body, what you will put on. Is not life more than food and the body more than clothing? Look at the birds in the air, for they neither sow nor reap nor gather into barns; yet*

your heavenly Father feeds them. Are you not of more value than they? Which of you by worrying can add one cubit to his stature? Therefore do not worry about tomorrow, for tomorrow will worry about its own things. Sufficient for the day is its own trouble," (Matthew 25-27,34).

To put it a different way, *"Courage does not always roar, sometimes it is a quiet voice at the end of the day, saying…"I will try again tomorrow,"* (Mary Anne Radmacker). There are reasons why God wants us to have courage:

1) God wants us to have courage in this life because we cannot reach our promise lands without it.

"Then shalt thou prosper, if thou takest heed to fulfil the statutes and judgments which the LORD charged Moses with concerning Israel: be strong, and of good courage; dread not, nor be dismayed."
(I Chronicles 22:13KJV)

Oftentimes we let fear and fretting delay our dreams. Occasionally, we may even blame God when we feel our prayers are not being answered. More often than not, it is our fears that keep us in the wilderness longer than we need to be, and our fears that keep us from stepping out on faith. Let us always be reminded that fear does not come from God - fear comes from the devil, and unfortunately, one of the devil's most common weapons against us is to immobilize us, and keep us from fulfilling our destinies by using fear.

The only way we can conquer fear is by not feeding it. Instead of fainting, we must not forget the power within us as Christians, and we must not forget that we are more than conquerors in Christ Jesus. While we are on our journeys waiting to reach our promise lands, we cannot fret about the length of time it takes to get there. Sometimes God purposely delays the timing. This delay is not to hurt us, but to prepare, define, shape and mold us. Subsequently, this allows us to witness His miracles and provisions in our lives so that when we reach our promise lands, we will have increased faith in Him and be equipped with everything we need to enjoy His blessings.

Shawn Callahan tells a story about a boy who was born without a right arm:

> On his ninth birthday he asked his parents if he could join a karate club. They were delighted by the idea and the boy quickly became a regular at the local dojo. The boy wanted to compete in a tournament and asked his master if this was possible. The master said he could but only if he listened carefully to his master and trusted him.
>
> The master taught the boy one move and one move only. The boy practiced it diligently but after a while he was worried that the other boys were learning a range of moves and he only had one. He asked the master to teach him other moves but the master said no. The master just urged the boy to keep practicing that one move.
>
> The boy won the first round of the tournament and then the next round and the one after that until he found himself winning the entire tournament. The boy was baffled. How did he do it? He asked the master how a boy with only one arm and only one move could win a karate tournament against these other boys. The master smiled and told the boy that there is only one defense against the move the boy learned and that defense involves grabbing the attacker by the right arm.

Our Master and Lord know our every weakness. Fortunately, God already has a remedy for any and every encounter we will have to face in life. Let's continue to trust God with the game plan of our lives and have courage and faith in Him.

2) God wants us to have courage because when we do it benefits others.

Courage is not the absence of fear but the inclusion of faith. It is impossible to have courage without faith. Faith and love drive out fear. It is out of love and courage that we then can help encourage and build the confidence of others. We can reassure others with absolute certainty of God's word found in II Corinthians 1:20 that, *"All the promises of God in Him are Yes, and in Him Amen, to the glory of God."* Also, *"God always leads us in triumph in Christ,"*.

When we have the courage and faith to follow God's commandments and be in God's perfect will for our lives, we benefit not only ourselves, but others as well. Scripture gives many examples of this spiritual truth. In Genesis 18, God tells Abraham that if he could find a certain number of righteous people in the city of Sodom that He would be willing to spare the whole place for their sake. Also, in Genesis 30:27, Laban urged Jacob not to return to his own country, *"Please stay, if I have found favor in your eyes," he said, "for I have learned by experience that the Lord has blessed me for your sake."* In addition, Genesis 39:5 says, *"The Lord blessed the Egyptian's house for Joseph's sake; and the blessing of the Lord was on all that he had in the house and in the field."*

These biblical examples of spiritual courage lead us to ask ourselves the question: How many people are we being a blessing to in our sphere of influence because of our acts of courage? Let us remember the good advice Andrew Jackson quoted, *"One man with courage makes a majority."*

3) God wants us to have courage because we then bring

glory to God

And David said to Solomon his son, Be strong and of good courage, and do it: fear not, nor be dismayed: for the LORD God, even my God, will be with thee; he will not fail thee, nor forsake thee, until thou hast finished all the work for the service of the house of the LORD," (I Chronicles 28:20).

Daniel had risen through the political ranks as an administrator of this pagan kingdom. Daniel had proven to be very honest and hardworking, and because of this, the other government officials were jealous of him. These officials wanted to remove Daniel from office, but could find nothing on him. So they tried to use Daniel's faith in God against him. The officials tricked King Darius into passing a decree that during a 30-day period, anyone who prayed to another god or man besides the king would be thrown into the Lion's Den. Daniel found out about the decree, but did not change his habits of going home, facing Jerusalem and kneeling to pray.

When they realized Daniel was not going to change his custom, they threw Daniel in the Lion's Den.

The king could not eat or sleep all night, and at dawn, ran to the Lion's Den, and asked Daniel if his God had protected him. Daniel replied, *"My God sent his angel, and he shut the mouths of the lions. They have not hurt me, because I was found innocent in his sight. Nor have I ever done any wrong before you, O king."* (Daniel 6:22) Scripture says the king was overjoyed. Daniel was brought out, unharmed, "*...because he had trusted in his God.*" (Daniel 6:23). Then the king issued another decree, ordering the people to fear and reverence the God of Daniel. Daniel prospered under the reign of Darius, and King Cyrus, the Persian after him.

Now because of Daniels' great courage, God was glorified! Just like the great example of Daniel we too can exhibit courage. Let's remember the poignant words of Martin Luther King Jr. who encourages us to "be a searcher for consensus and a molder of consensus."

7

TRUSTWORTHINESS / INTEGRITY

I know, my God, that you test the heart and are pleased with integrity. (I Chronicles 29:17)

When you see actions taken with integrity, instead of words only, you will then know a soul's worth (Shannon L. Alder)

God talks a lot about the subject of trustworthiness and integrity. These are some of the things that He has said.

God entrusts more to those who are trustworthy

But select capable men from all the people--men who fear God, trustworthy men who hate dishonest gain--and appoint them as officials over thousands, hundreds, fifties and tens, (Exodus 18:21)

I put Shelemiah the priest, Zadok the scribe, and a Levite named Pedaiah in charge of the storerooms and made Hanan son of Zakkur, the son of Mattaniah, their assistant, because they were considered trustworthy. They were made responsible for distributing the supplies to their fellow Levites, (Nehemiah 13:13)

When we are trustworthy over a few things God gives us more

Again, the Kingdom of Heaven can be illustrated by the story of a man going on a long trip. He called together his servants and entrusted his money to them while he was gone. He gave five bags of silver to one, two bags of silver to another, and one bag of silver to the last - dividing it in proportion to their abilities. He then left on his trip.

"The servant who received the five bags of silver began to invest the money and earned five more. The servant with two bags of silver also went to work and earned two more. But the servant who received the one bag of silver dug a hole in the ground and hid the master's money.

"After a long time their master returned from his trip and called them to give an account of how they had used his money. The servant to whom he had entrusted the five bags

of silver came forward with five more and said, 'Master, you gave me five bags of silver to invest, and I have earned five more.'

"The master was full of praise. 'Well done, my good and faithful servant. You have been faithful in handling this small amount, so now I will give you many more responsibilities. Let's celebrate together!'

"The servant who had received the two bags of silver came forward and said, 'Master, you gave me two bags of silver to invest, and I have earned two more.'

"The master said, 'Well done, my good and faithful servant. You have been faithful in handling this small amount, so now I will give you many more responsibilities. Let's celebrate together!'

"Then the servant with the one bag of silver came and said, 'Master, I knew you were a harsh man, harvesting crops you didn't plant and gathering crops you didn't cultivate. I was afraid I would lose your money, so I hid it in the earth. Look, here is your money back.'

"But, the master replied, 'You wicked and lazy servant! If you knew I harvested crops I didn't plant and gathered crops I didn't cultivate, why didn't you deposit my money in the bank? At least I could have gotten some interest on it.'

"Then, he ordered, 'Take the money from this servant, and give it to the one with the ten bags of silver. To those who *use well what they are given, even more will be given, and they will have an abundance. But from those who do nothing, even what little they have will be taken away*, (Matthew 25:14-29)

God wants women to be temperate and trustworthy

Their wives also must be of good character and must not gossip; they must be sober and honest in everything. (I Timothy 3:11)

The Lord hates lies and lack of integrity.

These are the things you are to do: Speak the truth to each other, and render true and sound judgment in your courts; do not plot evil against each other, and do not love to swear falsely. I hate all this," declares the LORD, (Zechariah 8:16-17)

Integrity means treating people fairly and honestly.

Do not use dishonest standards when measuring length, weight or quantity. Use honest scales and honest weights, an honest ephah and an honest hin. I am the LORD *your God, who brought you out of Egypt*, (Leviticus 19:35-36)

You must have accurate and honest weights and measures, so that you may live long in the land the LORD *your God is giving you* (Deuteronomy 25:15)

Honest scales and balances belong to the LORD; *all the weights in the bag are of his making. Kings detest wrongdoing, for a throne is established through righteousness. Kings take pleasure in honest lips; they value the one who speaks what is right* (Proverbs 16:11-13)

Your integrity should set an example

In everything set them an example by doing what is good. In your teaching show integrity, seriousness and soundness of speech that cannot be condemned, so that those who oppose you may be ashamed because they have nothing bad to say about us. (Titus 2:7)

It may be difficult to maintain your integrity

Then the LORD *said to Satan, "Have you considered my servant Job? There is no one on earth like him; he is blameless and upright, a man who fears God and shuns evil. And he still maintains his integrity, though you incited me against him to ruin him without any reason* (Job 2:3)

His wife said to him, "Are you still maintaining your integrity? Curse God and die!" He replied, "You are talking like a foolish woman. Shall we accept good from God, and not trouble?" (Job 2:9-10)

Integrity is more valuable than riches

Better the poor whose walk is blameless than the rich whose ways are perverse (Proverbs 28:6).

Integrity and uprightness protect me

May integrity and uprightness protect me, because my hope, LORD, is in you (Psalm 25:21)

He holds success in store for the upright, he is a shield to those whose walk is blameless, for he guards the course of the just and protects the way of his faithful ones (Proverbs 2:7-8)

Man with integrity walks securely

Whoever walks in integrity walks securely, but whoever takes crooked paths will be found out (Proverbs 10:9)

Your character can be corrupted by bad company

Do not be misled: Bad company corrupts good character (I Corinthians 15:33)

Integrity will be rewarded

As for you, if you walk before me faithfully with integrity of heart and uprightness, as David your father did, and do all I command and observe my decrees and laws, I will establish your royal throne over Israel forever, as I promised David your father when I said, 'You shall never fail to have a successor on the throne of Israel (I Kings 9:4-5)

I put in charge of Jerusalem my brother Hanani, along with Hananiah the commander of the citadel, because he was a man of integrity and feared God more than most people do (Nehemiah 7:2)

I know that you are pleased with me, for my enemy does not triumph over me. Because of my integrity you uphold me and set me in your presence forever (Psalm 41:11-12)

Several secular scholars and personalities have captured these same ideals as well. Two notable quotes below demonstrate this same theme:

THE WORLD NEEDS people… who cannot be bought whose word is their bond who put character above wealth who possess opinions and a will who are larger than their vocations who do not hesitate to take chances who will not lose their individuality in a crowd who will be as honest in small things as in great things who will make no compromise with wrong whose ambitions are not confined to their own selfish desires who will not say they do it "because everybody else does it" who are true to their friends through good report and evil report, in adversity as well as in prosperity who do not believe that shrewdness, cunning, and hardheadedness are the best qualities for winning success who are not ashamed or afraid to stand for the truth when it is unpopular who can say 'no' with emphasis, although all the rest of the world says 'yes' (Ted W. Engstrom)

People pay for what they do, and still more for what they have allowed themselves to become. And they pay for it very simply; by the lives they lead (James Baldwin)

As you can see, being trustworthy and having integrity is paramount to God. There is a direct link between integrity and God's willingness to use us for His greater glory. It is when we are willing participants in relinquishing our will to what God desires us to be that we witness the full extent of our blessings that God desires for us to have. Let us walk in the spirit with integrity so that our lives will be blessed and secure in the Lord.

ETIQUETTE / CONVERSATION

He who guards his lips guards his life, but he who speaks rashly will come to ruin (Proverbs 13:3)

The words we speak are merely an external verbalization to the internal discourse in our hearts. Our speech tells on us – giving away what is in our hearts, and our hearts reveal our true character. A recurring message that seems to apply to almost every area of temptation is guarding our lips/tongue by way of guarding our hearts. Let us take a look at some conversational etiquette do's and don'ts.

According to clinical psychologist Dr. Sophie Henshaw, "*Energy vampires are emotionally immature individuals who have the sense that the whole world revolves around them. They are almost incapable of seeing things from another person's perspective. They often lack empathy. They believe that they must take everything they can get from others and that giving anything will deprive them of essential resources. It's as if the whole world exists just to serve them and you are the latest object upon which they have set their sights for exploitation.*"

Energy Vampire Characteristics:

1) Those who monopolize the conversation

This person usually gives excessively long and repetitive background information about whatever they are talking about. Oftentimes you know every detail about their situation and/or family while they know nothing about yours.

The bible has this to say about Energy Vampires:

Whoever keeps his mouth and his tongue keeps himself out of trouble (Proverbs 21:23)

Do you see a man who is hasty in his words? There is more hope for a fool than for him (Proverbs 29:20)

Even a fool who keeps silent is considered wise; when he closes his lips, he is deemed intelligent (Proverbs 17:28)

2) Those who are not interested in what you have to say and always bring the conversation back to them

Several quotes from famous personalities speak very specifically about this person who is preoccupied with self:

"If I were to summarize in one sentence the single most important principle I have learned in the field of interpersonal relations, it would be this: Seek first to understand, then to be understood," - Stephen Covey

If *there is any one secret of success, it lies in the ability to get the other person's point of view and see things from his angle as well as your own,"* - Henry Ford

"What few people realize is that failure to be a good listener prevents us from hearing and retaining vital information, becoming a roadblock to personal and professional success," - Jean Marie Stine

"Most people do not listen with the intent to understand; they listen with the intent to reply," - Stephen Covey

The bible also speaks eloquently on this issue:

A fool finds no pleasure in understanding but delights in airing his own opinions (Proverbs 18:2)

Know this, my beloved brothers: let every person be quick to hear, slow to speak, slow to anger (James 1:19)

3) Those who are always complaining about something or someone (negative)

"The world of self-criticism on the one side and judgment toward others on the other side represents a major part of the dance of life." This quote by Hal and Sidra Stone sums up the toxic inner critic and inner defender mentality of those who frequently complain and criticize. The inner critic is an internal voice that judges us as inadequate. Oftentimes, this negative inner voice can find fault with anything relating to us such as, 1) our intellect, 2) our looks, 3) our personalities, 4) our abilities, 5) our perceptions of how others see us and, in severe cases, 6) a

sense of worthlessness.

On the other hand the inner defender, instead of judging ourselves, judges others. The inner defender may find fault and grumble about nearly any situation. The inner defender can be easily offended and hard to please. Maya Angelou said her grandmother would give her this advice, *"What you're supposed to do when you don't like a thing is change it. If you can't change it, change the way you think about it. Don't complain."*

The bible advises us as indicated below:

Do everything without complaining and arguing, so that no one can criticize you (Philippians 2:14a)

Don't grumble against one another, brothers and sisters, or you will be judged. The judge is standing at the door! (James 5:9)

4) Those who get easily offended

Could your hypersensitivity actually be robbing you of your joy? There are several signs of a person who might get offended easily and often:

- Are you angered easily over little things?
- Do others say you make big deals out of nothing?
- Do you often take things the wrong way?
- Do people feel they have to walk on eggshells around you?
- Do others consider you high maintenance?

Some secular scholars state the following about hypersensitivity:

"We should be too big to take offense and to noble to give it," - Abraham Lincoln.

"To be offended is a choice we make; it is not a condition inflicted or imposed upon us by someone or something else," - David A. Bednar

And the bible addresses this issue in the following verses:

He who covers over an offense promotes love, but whoever repeats the matter separates close friends (Proverbs 16:9)

Answer not a fool according to his folly, lest you be like him yourself (Proverbs 26:4)

For the sake of Christ, then, I am content with weaknesses, insults, hardships, persecutions, and calamities. For when I am weak, then I am strong (II Corinthians 12:10)

It is said when we find ourselves being easily offended we should turn to ourselves and look at our own faults and it will help us not get so angry.

5) Those who are "paranoid types"

According to Dr. Bruce Goldberg, *"These are soldiers still trying to win a war that no longer exists against an enemy that has long since perished. They do not trust anyone. Everyone is their enemy and life is their battleground. Fear is everywhere and an ingrained part of their personality makeup. Aggression is the most common response to the world from a paranoid type."*

There are many discussions on this topic, but two that stand out to me – one from the secular and one from the spiritual – are given below:

"You must change the way you talk to yourself about your life situations so that you no longer imply that anything outside of you is the immediate cause of your unhappiness. Instead of saying, 'Joe

makes me mad, say 'I make myself mad when I'm around Joe," - Ken Keyes.

"*Do not accuse a man for no reason- when he has done you no harm,*" (Proverbs 3:30)

6) Those who do not accept you as you are

"*To be fully seen by somebody, then, and be loved anyhow- this is a human offering that can border on miraculous,*" - Elizabeth Gilbert.

7) Those who use wounding words

"The way you use words has a tremendous impact on the quality of your life. Certain words are destructive; others are empowering," Susan Jeffers.

Do you see a man who speaks in haste? There is more hope for a fool than for him (Proverbs 30:20)

Starting a quarrel is like breaching a dam; so drop the matter before a dispute breaks out (Proverbs 17:14)

Whoever restrains his words has knowledge, and he who has a cool spirit is a man of understanding (Proverbs 17:27)

Reckless words pierce like a sword, but the tongue of the wise brings healing (to Proverbs 12:18)

Abstaining from barriers to effective verbal communication is imperative to having successful relationships. Some barriers to communicating include the following (Gordon, 1970):

1. <u>Criticizing</u> – When we constantly make negative judgments about others it causes other people around us to be on the defensive. Most people innately feel like they will be the next one on this negative evaluation chopping block. Consequently, other people will be reluctant to be transparent or vulnerable around people who criticize a lot in fear of themselves being rejected.

   Do not judge, or you too will be judged. For in the same way you judge others, you will be judged, and with the measure you use, it will be measured to you (Matthew 7:1-2).

2. <u>Name-calling and labeling</u> – The Lord commands that we guard our tongues.

But I say to you that everyone who is angry with his brother will be liable to judgment; whoever insults his brother will be liable to the council; and whoever says, 'you fool!' will be liable to the hell of fire

(Matthew 5:22)

Let no corrupting talk come out of your mouths, but only such as is good for building up, as fits the occasion, that it may give grace to those who hear (Ephesians 4:29)

3. <u>Advising negatively</u> – This is where people talk down to the other person while giving a solution to the problem. For example, someone might say "That's so easy to solve" or "That would not happen to me". The bible teaches us that *"the godly offers good counsel; they know right from wrong. They will fill their hearts with God's law, so they will never slip from His path"* (Psalm 37:30-31)

Let us look for wise godly counsel when seeking advice.

4. <u>Ordering/Threatening</u> – Some people try to control others by using idol threats or by commanding other people to do what they want.

But understand this, that in the last days there will come times of difficulty. For people will be lovers of self, lovers of money, proud, arrogant, abusive, disobedient to their parents, ungrateful, unholy, heartless, unappeasable, slanderous, without self-control, brutal, not loving good, treacherous, reckless, swollen with conceit, lovers of pleasure rather than lovers of God, having the appearance of godliness, but denying its power. Avoid such people. (II Timothy 3:1-5).

5. <u>Diverting</u> – This happens when people belittle other people's problems by comparing their problems to themselves. For example, they say things like, "You think your situation is bad let me tell you about my problems."

    This is what the bible teaches on this issue:

    Not that we dare to classify or compare ourselves with some of those who are commending themselves. But when they measure themselves by one another and compare themselves with one another, they are without understanding (II Corinthians 10:12)

    Philippians 4:8 tells us, "*Finally, brothers, whatever is true, whatever is right, whatever is pure, whatever is lovely, whatever is admirable — if anything is excellent or praiseworthy — think about such things."*

Let us look at each element of this phrase in detail:

1. <u>True</u> – This signifies everything that aligns with or agrees with the inherent truth which is the word of God (Scripture).
2. <u>Noble/Honest</u> – This signifies no lying, no falsehood and no hypocrisy. However, it encompasses embracing the qualities of righteousness, goodness, honor, virtuosity and living upright.
3. <u>Right/Just</u> – This signifies an opposition to all injustice, oppression, lack of respect or reverence to God or our fellow man. It means embracing the qualities of equitableness, living free from bias and upright, decent, proper and principled.
4. <u>Pure</u> – This signifies an opposition to all filthiness and foolish talking, obscene words and actions. It embraces the notion of being undefiled,

unpolluted and uncontaminated by the world. It exhibits a holiness of heart and life.

5. <u>Lovely</u> – This signifies an opposition to strife, wrath and contention. It embraces and cultivates love and amicableness among people.

6. <u>Admirable/ Good Report</u> – This signifies a good reputation, well spoken of, exemplary and a good name.

7. <u>Excellent/Virtue</u> – This signifies an opposition to immoral, criminal behavior, misconduct or bad personal character. It embraces good moral standards, integrity and honor.

8. <u>Praiseworthy</u> – This signifies being worthy of commendation, tribute and respect.

9

RESPECT

Show proper respect for everyone: Love the brotherhood of believers, fear God, honor the king (I Peter 2:7)

There is something respectable about people who know their identity and love themselves enough, and love the Lord enough, to accept and be who God made them. God wants us to be "first-class us" and not "second-class someone else". God has made us so individually unique for a reason, and to try to be a carbon-copy of someone else is not only insulting to God, but cheating God's purpose for our lives that only we can distinctively carry out.

As Shannon L. Alder stated,

"I existed on my own terms. I was different my entire life. Some called me divergent, others called me wild, crazy, unpredictable and unconformed—an apostate to the rules of the majority. I called myself God's creation and found purpose in the madness. When that day came, I didn't allow other people to dictate how I should feel or act. I learned there was no shame in imperfection because history had shown being different had the power to change perspectives and eventually the world. This is when I realized that flaws had responsibility. This was the day that I learned I was truly BLESSED!

In order to have respect for ourselves and develop this sense of identity, it has to come from the Source, which is God himself.

Let us take a look at how God sees His children:

1) We are created in God's image.

So God created man in his own image, in the image of God created he him; male and female created he them (Genesis 1:27)

From the beginning of the bible, God created both man and women in His image and placed them at the pinnacle of His creation. Both are equally beautiful and exalted above all other created beings.

2) We are heirs of God and joint-heirs with Christ.

And if children, then heirs; heirs of God, and joint-heirs with Christ; if so be that we suffer with Him, that we may be also glorified together (Romans 8:17)

This is the guarantee from God that, since the Holy Spirit is within us, we have a glorious inheritance that we share with Christ. This is an awesome privilege! Once we accepted Christ as our Lord and Savior, we gained all the rights and responsibilities of a child of God.

3) We are God's Temple.

And what agreement hath the temple of God with idols? For ye are the temple of the living God; as God hath said, I will dwell in them, and walk in them, and I will be their God, and they shall be my people (II Corinthians 6:16)

Know ye not that ye are the temple of God, and that the Spirit of

God dwelleth in you? (I Corinthians 3:16)

4) We are loved by God.

Who shall separate us from the love of Christ? Shall tribulation, or distress, or persecution, or famine, or nakedness, or peril, or sword? As it is written, "For Thy sake we are killed all the day long"; We are accounted as sheep for the slaughter. Nay, in all these things we are more than conquerors through Him that loved us. For I am persuaded, that neither death, nor life, nor angels, nor principalities, nor powers, nor things present, nor things to come, nor height, nor depth, nor any other creature, shall be able to separate us from the love of God, which is in Christ Jesus our Lord (Romans 8:35-39)

It is impossible to separate Christ's love from us! His death for us is proof of this undying love. We never have to fear that He has left us, no matter what difficulties or hardships we may face. His love is so great that we should always feel secure and never afraid.

5) We are important to God.

Wherefore, if God so clothed the grass of the field, which today is, and tomorrow is cast into the oven, shall He not much more clothe you, O ye of little faith? (Matthew 6:30)

Are not two sparrows sold for a farthing? And one of them shall not fall on the ground without your Father. But the very hairs on your head are all numbered. Fear ye not therefore, ye are of more value than many sparrows (Matthew 10:29-31)

God is very concerned about all aspects of our lives. We are more valuable to Him than any of His creations. Thankfully, because of the value that He places on His children, we do not need to worry when we face hardships and trials.

6) We are more than conquerors.

Nay in all these things we are more than conquerors through Him that loved us (Romans 8:37)

Oftentimes it seems that satan has won the victory over our situation. We must remember that Christ turned satan's apparent victory into defeat when He conquered death through the resurrection. This is the assurance that nothing we face can ever defeat us – we will always be victorious in Christ.

Since we know that God not only loves us but values us let us see how we can value ourselves by showing respect for ourselves.

1) Show respect for self

   a) <u>Proverbs 11:16 – kind hearted women gain respect.</u>

   "Compassion is the ultimate and most meaningful embodiment of emotional maturity. It is through compassion that a person achieves the highest peak and deepest reach in his or her search for self-fulfillment." - Arthur Jersild

   When we are in a position to treat a person anyway we wish, and we choose to treat the person with kindness, gentleness and respect, we are not only operating in the Fruit of the Spirit, but we are in God's perfect will. There are so many ways to show kindness. Offering not only a kind word but a kind deed goes a long way. Some examples: giving a tired mom a break by offering to baby-sit, lending an ear to someone in distress, baking cookies or contacting someone to let them know you are thinking about them, fixing dinner for someone who just had surgery, giving and serving the least of these.

Oftentimes, kindness is rarely random but purposeful. Let us purpose in our hearts to act in kindness.

b) <u>I Timothy 3:11-12 – women and men worthy of respect.</u>

Being competent at what you do gains respect. Competence happens when there is a continuous study or training of a certain area of knowledge, or a skill that gives you the ability to do something well. King Solomon had a heart that valued knowledge and wisdom. King Solomon was considered the wisest king to have ever lived. However, Solomon understood that his wisdom and sufficiency came from the Lord. *"Not that we are competent in ourselves to claim anything for ourselves, but our competence comes from God,"* (II Corinthians

3:5, ESV). Also, James 1:5 tells us, *"If any of you lacks wisdom, you should ask God, who gives generously to all without finding fault, and it will be given to you."*

In addition, a person gains respect by honoring their word and letting their word be bond. One thing that causes people to lose respect of you quickly is when they feel they cannot trust you or count on you. *"All you need to say is simply 'Yes' or 'No'; anything beyond this comes from the evil one,"* (Matthew 5:37).

Additionally, harsh words and gossip not only tarnishes the reputation of the person you are talking about but it taints and pollutes the appearance of the person who is doing the bad mouthing. More specifically, respect is given to those who are a role model to others and inspire others to reach their highest level of God given potential. Titus 2:1-8 says, *"You, however, must teach what is appropriate to sound doctrine. Teach the older men to be temperate, worthy of respect, self-controlled, and sound in faith, in love and in endurance. Likewise, teach the older women to be reverent in the way they live, not to be slanderers or addicted to much wine, but to teach what is good. Then they can urge the younger women to love their husbands and children, to be self-controlled and pure, to be busy at home, to be kind, and to be subject to their husbands, so that no one will malign the word of God. Similarly, encourage the young men to be self-controlled. In everything set them an example by doing what is good. In your teaching show integrity, seriousness and soundness of speech that cannot be condemned, so that those who oppose you may be ashamed because they have nothing bad to say about us.*

2) Show respect to others:

a) <u>Leviticus 19:32 – Respect for elderly.</u>

Stand up in the presence of the elderly and show respect for the aged. Fear your God. I am the LORD. (Leviticus 19:32)

Likewise, you who are younger, be subject to the elders. Clothe yourselves, all of you, with humility toward one another, for "God opposes the proud but gives grace to the humble (I Peter 5:5)

Honor your father and your mother, that your days may be long in the land that the Lord your God is giving you (Exodus 20:12)

Never speak harshly to an older man, but appeal to him respectfully as you would to your own father. Talk to younger men as you would to your own brothers. Treat older women as you would your mother, and treat younger women with all purity as you would your own sisters. Take care of any widow who has no one else to care for her. (Timothy 5:1-3)

Then King Rehoboam consulted the elders who had served his father Solomon during his lifetime. "How would you advise me to answer these people?" he asked." (I Kings 12:6)

In all of these scriptural examples, it is clear that God wants us to respect the elderly. Many countries such as China and India hold the elderly in very high esteem. Unfortunately, for the U.S., it is just the opposite. America puts a high respect and adoration for the youthful. Although both the young and the old are important in a healthy society, having a youth oriented mentality and elevating the youth to a higher position in society above the elderly goes against what God teaches. We should all remember whether we are young or old what James 4:14 says, *"You are just a vapor that appears for a little while and then vanishes away."* As my grandmother use to say, "Just keep on living."

b. <u>Ephesians 5:33 – Women respect husband/Husband love wife.</u>

Nevertheless let every one of you in particular so love his wife even as himself; and the wife [see] that she reverence [her] husband. (Ephesians 5:33)

Submitting yourselves one to another in the fear of God. (Ephesians 5:21)

Likewise, ye wives, [be] in subjection to your own husbands; that, if any obey not the word, they also may without the word be won by the conversation of the wives; (I Peter 3:1-6)

But I would have you know, that the head of every man is Christ; and the head of the woman [is] the man; and the head of Christ [is] God. (I Corinthians 11:3)

Husbands, love [your] wives, and be not bitter against them. (Colossians 3:19)

Likewise, ye husbands, dwell with [them] according to knowledge, giving honour unto the wife, as unto the weaker vessel, and as being heirs together of the grace of life; that your prayers be not hindered. (I Peter 3:7)

Let the husband render unto the wife due benevolence: and likewise also the wife unto the husband. (I Corinthians 7:3)

God designed the beautiful union of marriage between the man and the woman. However, the enemy is always lurking at the doorstep, trying to wreak havoc on the marriage and family relationship. Fortunately, the Lord has given some biblical prescriptions for a married couple to live by.

Respect is very important to men and God knew this; that is why God told women to respect their husbands. We can respect our husbands by the things we say to them, how we say it and our actions. Also, I noticed the bible does not say *respect your husband only if he is deserving.* On the contrary, the bible says *"if any obey not the word, they also may without the word be won by the conversation of the wives."* God calls us to *"Let all bitterness, and wrath, and anger, and clamour, and evil speaking, be put away from you, with all malice,"* (Ephesians 4:31). Let us love and respect each other through the help of the Holy Spirit and God's Word.

c. <u>1 Thessalonians 5:12-13 – Respect those who work hard among you.</u>

Now we ask you, brothers and sisters, to acknowledge those who work hard among you, who care for you in the Lord and who admonish you. Hold them in the highest regard in love because of their work. Live in peace with each other. (I Thessalonians 5:12-13)

The soul of the sluggard craves and gets nothing, while the soul of the diligent is richly supplied. (Proverbs 13:4)

Go to the ant, O sluggard; consider her ways, and be wise. Without having any chief, officer, or ruler, she prepares her bread in summer and gathers her food in harvest. (Proverbs 6:6-8)

The hand of the diligent will rule, while the slothful will be put to forced labor. (Proverbs 12:24)

For even when we were with you, we would give you this command: If anyone is not willing to work, let him not eat. For we hear that some among you walk in idleness, not busy at work, but busybodies. Now such persons we command and encourage in the Lord Jesus Christ to do their work quietly and to earn their own living. (II Thessalonians 3:10-12)

In all toil there is profit, but mere talk tends only to poverty. (Proverbs 14:23)

and to aspire to live quietly, and to mind your own affairs, and to work with your hands, as we instructed you, so that you may walk properly before outsiders and be dependent on no one. (I Thessalonians 4:11-12)

In the same way, let your light shine before others, so that they may see your good works and give glory to your Father who is in heaven. (Matthew 5:6)

Whoever works his land will have plenty of bread, but he who follows worthless pursuits lacks sense. (Proverbs 12:11)

Then he said to his disciples, "The harvest is plentiful, but the laborers are few. (Matthew 9:37)

Oftentimes we may work with people who are not honorable and may have a lack of character; nevertheless, we must operate with respect, and remember that we are not working for man but we are working unto the Lord.

Regardless of whether we get adequately rewarded at work, or made to feel appreciated, let us allow our good works shine though, and be a testimony for others to see, so that God will get the ultimate glory. God sees our diligence, and He will reward us accordingly and be pleased with us.

Additionally, we know that there is so much kingdom work to be done and not a lot of laborers. Let us be a blessing to those who sacrifice and work hard in the faith and let us purpose in our hearts to be co-laborers in Christ.

Made in the USA
Columbia, SC
03 July 2017